BLACK VALUES MATTER

An Essay On How To Improve Baltimore And Black America

BERNARD (BERNEY) FLOWERS
Lieutenant Colonel
US Air Force (Retired)

Copyright © 2022 by Bernard (Berney) Flowers

ISBN: 978-1-64810-212-7

All rights reserved. No part of this book may be reproduced mechanically, electronically, virtually, or by any other means, including photocopying without written permission of the publisher. It is illegal to copy this book, post it to any website or distribute it by any other means without permission from the publisher.

Published by Perfect Publishing Co.

"He Who Is Not Courageous Enough To Take Risks Will Accomplish Nothing In Life"

— *Muhammad Ali*

DEDICATION

To my dear wife Carolyn, thanks for being my girlfriend and partner in crime for over three decades. May we have three more decades of love, health and happiness together.

To Hillary, Jon, Manny and Violet: Everything I do is with you in mind. I love you and I am eternally proud of you.

To Armond and Martha Pearl Flowers, my parents: I miss you. May you rest in peace.

ACKNOWLEDGEMENTS

To my campaign team: Mr. Hollis Albert, Mrs. Beth Lawson, Mr. Will Lawson, Dr. Ray Serrano and Ms. Kira Wynne. What a fun journey we had. We learned a lot together. Let's do it again soon?

To My Editors And Reviewers: Lieutenant Colonel Cail Morris (Ret), Ms. Linda McCluney, Ms. Angela Lane, Dr. Frank Nice, Dr. Eric Clemons, Dr. (Lieutenant Colonel) Scott Willens (Ret), Ms. Blanca Tapahuasco, Ms. Donna Rzepka, Ms. Lori Crabb, and Dr. Ken Rochon (my publisher) thank you all for your steadfast, support and guidance. Whether you agreed with my sentiments or not, your opinions and critiques helped me greatly. This book would not have happened without you.

FOREWORD

I am Vince Crabb. Berney is one of my lifelong best friends. We traveled all over America together, all over the Middle East together, and we were even mortared and shot at together. We are "Battle Buddies", which means, we have each other's back, no matter what, even all these years after our military service. You will find no greater friend than Berney. I am proud that he asked me to say a few words about him in his newest adventure.

I hope you enjoy my friend's book.

"Ready? Let's Roll!!!"

Vincent D. Crabb,
Colonel, US Army (Ret),
The ORIGINAL "Sheriff Of Baghdad"

PREFACE

I love America. I have spent significant time outside it. My time outside this country makes me appreciate it even more. To me, love includes telling the truth, even when it hurts. Too many Americans are not living as they want to and deserve to. There is enough prosperity, comfort, goodness, liberty and freedom for all in this grand experiment of a country. When goodness is not shared fairly, according to the labors of the individual, historically "the natives get restless".

Some of our brothers and sisters are not getting their fair share of the American Dream. Our government and corporations are leaving some people behind. Some Americans are suffering from "a lack of knowledge". My intention in writing this book is to share my limited experiences in order that more Americans might pursue and secure the blessings of liberty.

I say some controversial things in this essay. My hope is that you will read the whole book before you judge it.

Table of Contents

Chapter 1: WHAT'S THE PROBLEM WITH BALTIMORE
AND OUR URBAN CENTERS? 1
   Charm City Is Hurting 2
   Why Are Baltimoreans Angry? 4
   Please Don't Tell Martin! 7

Chapter 2: BLACK CULTURE IS UNDER ATTACK 13
   Are Blacks Racists? 13
   The Media Controls Our Image 16
   Daniel Patrick Moynihan and "The Woman King" ... 19
   Has Feminism Helped "The Struggle"? 23
   Squeegee Boys - Menace Or Blessing? 25

Chapter 3: POLITICS, CHURCHES AND BIG MONEY 27
   How Can Black People Lead America In Both Church
   Attendance And Negative Social Statistics? 27
   Churches Got COVID (PPP) Money. Where Is It? ... 28
   Is Drag Queen Story Time Good For Our Children? ... 32
   What Have They Done For You Lately? 34
   Why Do We Tolerate Poor Governance? 36
   Why Do We Tolerate Poor Leaders? 40

Would Republicans Be Any Better? 43

What Did President Obama Give Us For Our Votes? 45

Where Are My Reparations? 51

Black Churches Got "What" From President Obama?............53

Did President Obama Support "Black Values"
Or LGBTQ Values? 55

African Americans, Black Americans and Jesse Jackson:
What Is Our Allegiance To The Slave Catchers? 56

The Ashanti Tribe 60

Why Are The Elites Bringing In So Many Refugees and
Migrants? 62

Yes, Black Votes Matter 70

Chapter 4: HOW DID WE GET TO THIS POINT?....................73

Our Grandparents, Their Parents And Your Parents
Were Conservatives..73

Reconstruction and the South..76

Why Did President Harry Truman Desegregate The
Military? 78

Chapter 5: HOW WE FIX BALTIMORE
(And Inner-City America)..81

Let's Put The Charm Back In Charm City 81

Let's Treat Our Fellow Humans As We Want To Be Treated.84

Homeless Baltimore 87

Let's Reform Our Police..89

Should We Bring In The National Guard? 90

What Have the Democrat's Done for Baltimore Lately? 93

Let's Fix Our Schools...94
Let's Take Charge Of Our Children's Educations...................98
Can The Republicans Be More Inclusive?...........................98
Let's Keep Smiling..102

SUMMARY (The Beginning Of Better Days).......................105

ACKNOWLEDGEMENTS..107

MORE FROM BERNEY...109

REFERENCES 111

Endnotes..123

Chapter 1

WHAT'S THE PROBLEM WITH BALTIMORE AND OUR URBAN CENTERS?

"I would unite with anybody to do right and with nobody to do wrong."

— *Frederick Douglass*

"...And in the eyes of the people, there is the failure; and in the eyes of the hungry, there is a growing wrath. In the souls of the people, the grapes of wrath are filling and growing heavy, growing heavy for the vintage."

— *John Steinbeck.*

America's urban centers are dying. Chicago, Detroit, Atlanta, New Orleans, Los Angeles, New York...they are all becoming unlivable. I have resided in Maryland for the last fourteen years, so I will use Baltimore as a working model to address the decay in America's urban centers. Most of these urban centers are dominated socially and politically by Black Americans.

Charm City Is Hurting

I read the Baltimore Sun daily. In it, almost every day, a death is reported. I am not talking about accidents. I am talking about crime. I am talking about premature deaths. I am talking about lives being cut short, not only by crime, but by culture and values. There was a recent story of a teenaged girl who was shot by an adolescent boy who somehow got hold of his security guard Mom's loaded gun. It went off as he played with it, and a promising 15-year-old lost her life.[1]

A friend who lives in Baltimore called me in a panic on a recent Sunday morning. As she was on her way to church, living in the heart of the city, she went out to her car and discovered a dead body. She called the police. Two hours later, as they had not arrived, she called me. She was frantic and had no other place to turn. I tried to calm her nerves as best as I could, talking to her until the police arrived an hour later.

I am not faulting the police. Although it took them three hours to administer to that dead body, they have been ridiculed and attacked in a way that is unprecedented in my memory. "Defund the Police" campaigns have peppered the city. As a result, peace officers are leaving the police force in droves, leaving the city missing more than 800 Peace Officers at the time of the writing of these words.

Another recent incident involved one of the local "Squeegee Boys," otherwise known as the "extortionists", who come up to cars in the city supposedly washing car windows for "donations". One "Squeegee Boy" shot and killed a man recently. This man happened to be a married father with three kids…a tax paying Maryland citizen who worked in the city. As he was approached, he simply had

CHAPTER 1

enough of the Squeegee Boys daily extortion tactics. After a verbal exchange, he left his car to chase the perpetrator with a baseball bat. Of course that was the wrong thing to do. This perpetrator pulled out a gun and shot the man to death. Now another family is without its father. More kids are missing their dad. Another widow joins the long line of unhappy women who are alone and don't want to be.

HBO's "The Wire" and "We Own This City" are TV shows that depict the violence and everyday corruption that Americans who live in the city must deal with every day. In the supposed "Land of the Free and Home of the Brave", Americans should be able to go about their daily lives without fear or intimidation. That is not the case in many parts of Baltimore. Somehow, all of this has gotten out of whack. It needs to change.

My intention with this book is to identify the root cause of all this pain in Baltimore and America's urban areas, and offer practical solutions to solve these problems. My solutions will not be popular but if implemented, they will be effective. The alternative is… THE STATUS QUO…the same crime, bad living conditions… No Change. Just lower and lower standards and "more and more" poverty. "More and more" despair.

I believe that one day, I will read the Baltimore Sun and see my vision: fewer major crimes, no homicides and no premature death. Until that vision occurs, we have work to do. Until that vision becomes reality, we should be working toward improving our lives and the lives of our fellow citizens.

Who am I to think that I can fix all this? I am a retired career military officer with time spent in several war zones. After retiring from the Air Force, I spent over thirteen years as a senior civil servant working in leadership roles in the Federal Interagency. I know what works in government. I know what doesn't work. I believe that our country's best days are still in front of us, but we need to change the direction of the country now before it's too late.

Over the past few years, I saw our government do some things that I wasn't comfortable with, so I decided that I personally should try to make a positive change in the direction of our government and our nation. I believe in "walking the talk", as they say, so I left my cushy civil service job seeking to make a bigger difference "outside the fence". I ran for office recently and failed. However, I remain undeterred. I have a plan to make things better. With Divine Providence and your help, maybe we can improve the lives of all Americans, and especially those living in the inner city.

Why Are Baltimoreans Angry?

Testimonials

> *"Sometimes, I feel like I'm in another world in Baltimore City. During the first year and even partially of the second year after all this began, I was not getting mail regularly. Once I went to the Post Office on Eastern Ave. to ask for my mail because I needed a letter with pertinent patient information, and I asked the mail person out front to help me because I did not get mail for about 3 weeks. She refused to check in the back of the Post Office for me. I identified myself as a doctor and let her know it involved medical information that I needed. She told me to wait at the end and the manager would speak with me. When the manager came out, I was not greeted. I was yelled at, and*

CHAPTER 1

she asked who told me to talk to her. I politely explained the situation and she assisted me". — **Dr. Joe**

On Mother's Day, my wife and I had a reservation at Fogo De Chao, a fancy Brazilian Steak House in downtown Baltimore. The city was busy with families just leaving their respective churches and looking to celebrate the day. My wife wanted to use valet parking, so we pulled into a line of cars waiting for valet service. We were about fifteen cars away from the valet stand. We waited patiently. All was well.

While we were in the queue, waiting to drop off our car, I noticed a huge black suburban wheeling up behind us. The woman in the suburban was dressed as if she had just left church. She was alone. Perhaps she had dropped off passengers at the entrance to the restaurant? She was right beside us. She had the familiar, angry look of competitive self-righteousness…as if she felt entitled to cut the line. She drove her huge tank of a truck, slowly passing each vehicle in the line, looking for a someone to make eye contact with her, and weak enough to let her cut the line. Why couldn't she patiently and civilly wait in line, like the rest of us? Didn't she just leave church? Why did she feel so entitled? Fat lot of good church did her? This woman was dead set on forcing her way into that line.

We sat there for about fifteen minutes. I was not going to make room for her, but in truth, none of the people in line could have let her in to the line had they wanted to. We simply could not move our vehicles. Eventually, she paralleled the line of cars and nudged the bumper of her giant SUV into the very front of the queue.

Assuming this pushy woman had just gotten out of church, in my mind I asked, "what would Jesus do" in this situation? I asked because I notice a mental ugliness that permeates Baltimore. Heading north on I-95, once you cross the Patapsco River, people seem to get just a little more aggressive…a little more angry. Everyone seems to be on edge. Is that why there are so many shootings and killings in the city?

Back to reality; what about the rest of the people who had patiently waited in line? As one of the people in the line, I was not happy. I am sure that my line mates weren't either. I'm sure they felt somewhat put upon. My guess is that they took their frustrations out on someone else later that day.

Emotions can be shared between people like a virus. What is important is what emotions we choose to share. We can choose to share joyous emotions or we can choose to share negative emotions. In this case, this woman chose to share negative emotions by aggressively forcing her way into the line of cars. As a result, she ruined our experience and probably that of the many people who were in the queue of cars with us. The restaurant lost the money my wife and I would have spent. The waiters missed the tip we would have left. The city lost the tax revenue we would have left. We cancelled our reservation and went to another restaurant in the suburbs. Who knows what the other people in line chose to do? Perhaps they took the incident in stride? Perhaps they went out and spread negativity to the next person they encountered?

On another recent visit to Baltimore, I witnessed huge swarms of dirt bike riders lawlessly racing up and down the streets of the Inner Harbor. These swarms of riders showed no respect for pedestrians or traffic laws. I saw one rider pop a wheelie roughly fifty yards before his next traffic light. He skillfully and impressively maintained his front tire in the air as he went through the red light at twenty miles per hour. There was no police presence in sight. Restaurant and bar patrons standing on the street corner with me were visibly unnerved and probably will go home telling the story of how rough Baltimore is. They probably won't come back.

Negativity spreads like a virus. It has spread all over the city and it's not going anywhere soon unless we change the way we treat each other. The common denominator in these stories is that of some Black Americans act as if our culture has no values or civility.

Please Don't Tell Martin!

Thank you, Ms. Coretta, for the grace, strength, and dignity that you displayed.

Since your wonderful husband was assassinated by the bullets of fear and hate.

You know they killed him because of their ignorance.

Thank you for not allowing bitterness and anger to engulf your very existence.

Now that you are reunited with Martin, tell him that they are stripping our rights away, day by day, but his fight was not in vain.

Tell him that although my generation glorifies drugs, debases black women in song, and calls us vulgar names – that his dream still remains.

Our men no longer celebrate our natural black beauty – we have to have long weaves, small waists, and big ole booties.

The videos are so degrading, they mirror soft porn.

Us Blacks own television stations now, but that's all that's shown.

Tell Martin that my generation apologizes for its lack of respect for his legacy and the dormancy of our elders; we might as well call this the Civil Rights of Unmovement Era.

Tell him that although we as black people make more than we've ever seen, that we squander it on diamond clad teeth, 24-inch rims, and designer clothes due to our sagging self-esteem.

Tell Martin that our babies are growing up without fathers, while the mothers are catching buses just like he remembers.

Our children take to the streets in droves, not to march or proclaim the injustice of this nation, but to pledge their gang affiliation.

I can't rhyme to this next line. On any night thugs hang out while bullets ring out – not freedom.

And yes, we continue to be judged by the color of our skin by America but I wonder most about the lack of the content of our character.

Advise him that the grand-daughters of the Civil Rights era are making their money as strippers.

CHAPTER 1

The grand-sons of the marchers are ignoring their sons and daughters and hanging and slinging on corners.

They're going to jail in mass numbers, not for protesting, marching, or defying racism, but because they commit illegal acts to gain materialism.

Our children are making babies, ignoring education, committing felonious capers, I'd wish they'd read his Birmingham Jail Papers.

Tell Martin that those in the ghetto are not the only ones forgetting his dream.

There are those who've forgotten where they came from because of a little cream.

Who refuse to give back to the community, because their motto is 'More for me'

They've forgotten how to lend a helping hand, to help their fellow man – all the while thinking, 'If I can make it, they can.'

Looking down without offering a leg up, getting on elevators with their noses up.

Some of us are even Republicans now, but that's a very exclusive black crowd.

Striving to get to the top of the ladder, to make their pockets fatter – instead of doing something that truly matters.

Leaving the 'hood' in droves and only moving back when Whites buy up all of the homes.

Tell Martin that we still like to dance and sing, but not Negro spirituals cuz we've got Beyonce grinding and shaking her thing.

Ms. Coretta, this may hurt poor Martin the most – it just may seal the deal, we as a people don't attend church anymore.

Cuz we've gotten a little education and found out that God wasn't real.

For those of us who still believe, it makes us want to holler, we've got a pimp named Bishop and a Bishop named Dollar.

I don't know Ms. Coretta, maybe you'd better not tell Martin that for all that he's done to make us free, equal, and just – that we still migrate to the back of the bus. I'll bet looking down – he doesn't recognize us.

We've forgotten how to march, protest, and vote - but be at the club, standing in line for hours – in the freezing cold.

Sporting the latest gear; stilettos, hoochie clothes, teeth that's froze, and Tims – driving cars with less tire more rim. Dying to get in so that we can 'shake it fast', drop it like it's hot' – forgetting the respect and dignity that we were taught.

I never thought I'd think this thought, but please don't even give Martin your report.

CHAPTER 1

Ms. Coretta, maybe you should just avoid mentioning my generation all together.

~By Bitter Bitch. [2]

Chapter 2
BLACK CULTURE IS UNDER ATTACK

Are Blacks Racists?

There is an old Chris Rock comedy routine. It's one of my favorites. Basically, he says;

> "There's a civil war going on with Black people, and there's two sides: there's Black people and there's Niggas. The Niggas have got to go." "I love Black People, but I hate Niggas." "It's not White people that are breaking into your house to steal your new big screen TV. It's Niggas."[3]

Just like Chris says, "there is a civil war going on with Black people"...and we are ALL losing.

Are African Americans perpetrating a fraud? Many of us are quick to pull the race card at the slightest provocation, when we should be thinking to give individual people the benefit of the doubt? Perhaps we should try to set the racial example before we pull the "race card"? I read stories about wealthy and upper middle class Black kids attending elite colleges, insisting and expecting the college to create Black-only dorms [4]. Isn't that the epitome of hypocrisy? Separatism isn't what MLK worked so hard for. Last I checked, there were plenty of HBCU's (Historically Black College or University) with all-Black dorms that these mostly elite kids could attend. But they choose not to because they really don't want to be around poor and middle-class Blacks. They want to brag about attending elite schools. They also prefer to be around their privileged, social-climbing counter-parts from other ethnicities. To me, this behavior is the epitome of hypocrisy.

A great man once said, "A House Divided Will Not Stand." Black Americans are terribly divided and we are not standing together. Why do Blacks lead the nation in negative social statistics? Why do we allow corporate and government elites to pit us against each other. Have you heard of the "Woman King" [5] movie? The real truth is that the Dahomey Tribe were the biggest enslavers of their African neighbors. As long as we continue to see each other as enemies, only the elites will prosper.

Among my ethnicity, I hear people referring to each other as "Kings and Queens". I have news for those folks, there can be only one "King". There can be only one "Queen". Most social structures are hierarchical. Even the Dahomey women warriors had a King that they served. And for those who champion Marxism and Communism as solutions to our problems, I recommend they take a look at the current Chinese Communist leadership structure. They will find it hierarchical, just like it is in the western world. In the West under Capitalism, there is freedom to rise up the social ladder and "live your best life". Under Communism, if you rise too far, or too fast, unless you come from a protected family, you will be quickly reminded that your ass belongs to the state. Ask refugees and immigrants who fled countries like Cambodia, Vietnam,

China, Russia, etc. They will happily tell you how life was under Communism and why they came to America.

I count Nigerians, Ghanaians, Ugandans and other foreigners among my friends. These are men that I served with. Several of them and their families quietly marvel at how "African Americans" act so entitled and spend so much time complaining about their country while most immigrants see America as the "land of opportunity". They call African Americans "Sons of Slaves" behind our backs. I know other Americans from Asia, Central and South America who feel the same way. Many of these folks entered this country as non-English speakers and within a generation are proudly sending their children to America's elite colleges. Having traveled all over this planet, I can say that there is no other place I would rather live, warts and all.

Back to the question: Are Blacks racists? Honestly, I believe that all humans are somewhat racist, including me. However, my military service and spiritual background have forced me to adjust my personal biases. Our military socializes its members towards building successful teams. We were taught to subsume our biases for the greater good.

For those of you progressives who are cursing me for my blasphemous statements, please answer this question: can you find me a country or an ethnic group that isn't racist? Most countries are made of ethnically homogenous people. Try immigrating to Japan or China or North Korea? Even woke Canada has a stricter immigration policy than America. America is sometimes referred to as "The Great Melting Pot". Everyone is welcomed here, as long as our immigration rules are followed. I digress; if we work to overcome our individual biases, perhaps we can become better people, presenting ourselves to be more pleasing to our Creator and to each other while building a more libertarian, more tolerant, LESS WOKE society in the process. So, **is Racism a Black Value? Are Black Americans Racists? Are YOU a racist?**

The Media Controls Our Image

Years ago, I was driving east on the German Autobahn. Driving pedal to metal in my rented BMW was exhilarating as there was no speed limit traveling between Spangdahlem and Stuttgart. I had my radio blasting a great station that played American music. It was the early 2000's and a rap song came on that frankly, startled me. The lyrics spoken by a clearly Black American female rapping, "My Neck, My Back, My Pussy and My Crack".[6] As a proud service member representing my nation overseas, I was embarrassed to hear that song on the open airwaves. I wondered what other ethnic groups thought of Black Americans who would produce such vulgar lyrics? More importantly, who paid to produce this song? I doubt the producers were Black people. Let's not even bring up Cardi B, Megan Thee Stallion and Niki Minaj. They appear to be real "paragons of virtue".

I love me some "Tribe Called Quest". I love most rap music. Starting with the Sugar Hill Gang, all the way up to Snoop Dogg, Dr. Dre, Eminem and Kendrick Lamar, I love it. Like Blues and Jazz, it's an American cultural art form. Rap tells the story of America's Black community, warts and all. But the problem is that our story has just too many warts.

When I was young, Grandmaster Flash and the Furious Five released "The Message".[7] It told tales of what was happening in the New York streets. It told about the pressure that a young Black man faces growing up in a caustic, urban environment. As real as it was, there was no cursing…no denigrating of our Black Women… and, the word "Nigga" was not used.

What was intended as an ugly term of denigration was transformed into a "term of endearment" by hip hop groups like "Public Enemy". I will even admit to calling some of my closest friends, "Nigga", in the past. I have even heard young White kids call each other Nigga. Dave Chappelle, the comic genius who has become the leading philosopher of his time, uses the word profusely…and I enjoy it greatly when he does.

There is a cost to be paid for the use of the word. We have created a two-class system where Blacks can use the word and others can't. It's illogical. If I call my homeboy, Nigga, he might say back to me, "Fuck you, Nigga." To us, the word is an acknowledgement of our masculine friendship, as we both smile.

We must account for the idea that media, who hates Blacks by the way, profits from "The Struggle". Years ago, Bob Johnson's Black Entertainment Television (BET) was a proud, uplifting outlet for the promotion of Black American culture. Since it was purchased by VIACOM Corporation, BET appears to promote only the worst of our culture with "hip hop hoes" endlessly twerking and weak-assed Tyler Perry movies shown, ad-nauseum. An entire generation has grown up thinking that BET represents the whole of Black culture. All the while, BET's profits are enjoyed by the VIACOM media cartel, which by its programing, demonstrates its hatred of Black Americans. So, our image was sold to "the man" and today is controlled by people who hate us. Our Black musical artists make music that encourages the destruction of the Black American community.

Years ago, one of my dearest war buddies used the phrase "Alabama Porch Monkey" in a sentence where I could hear it. He just happened to be from America's racial majority. I was livid. I was incensed. How could a dear friend of mine use such a derogatory phrase? I took the time to correct him as to why that was an inappropriate phrase to use. Although that event happened in 1988, I surely came off as some whacked out diversity counsellor. The shame is that when I got with my Black friends later, we proudly called each other 'Nigga', using the term as a badge of honor.

Why was it OK for me to use the term Nigga in my speech with my Black friends? Why is it OK for OutKast to use the term Nigga profusely in its music? Why does it sound so terrible for my majority friend to even reference Black people in a less than positive way, even when it's deserved? As a thinking man, it seems odd that I can say Nigga but my Irish/Italian friend can't say it, even thirty-four years later. Am I a hypocrite? Is "Nigga" a term of endearment? For some people, it is and for some people, it isn't. But, either way, can Black American's not critique our speech and behavior?

Four-hundred years of slavery and oppression probably has a little to do with why I feel anger when my Irish/Italian buddy uses that ethnic slur. It sounds great to me when the Wu Tang Clan's says it. There is a clear dichotomy here.

Maybe the only group who can solve that dichotomy is Black Americans? As comfortable as it feels when it slips off the tongue, perhaps Black Americans should cut back on the use of the word, especially around our youth. I will admit that I have used the word in the past. But it is sometimes a curse word for Black Americans, and we should try to not curse around our kids, lest we be infected with the same moral and verbal weakness that afflicts my generation. Most spiritual people know that life and death is in the power of the tongue. You can choose to speak blessings or curses. Black people are just as racist as the people who we accuse of racism. As such, we have no moral high ground to stand upon. Maybe we are just hypocrites who should strive to set the example by not demonstrating racist behavior.

Daniel Patrick Moynihan and "The Woman King"

Earlier, I mentioned a new movie called "The Woman King"[8]. I have not seen the movie, nor will I ever see it. From what I glean from its promos, it tells a propagandized "real life" story of an all-female regiment of warriors which existed from the late 1600s to the mid-1800s' in what was once the West African kingdom of Dahomey. I won't see the movie because I am certain that it will tell a woke, fictionalized tale of invincible, Black Amazon warriors who were fearless in battle and absolutely dominated all "male warriors they encountered". I won't see the movie because I'm certain that the woke, blonde feminist movie producers, Maria Bello and Cathy Schulman, who sanctioned this revisionist history, won't tell you the documented truth of what really happened. The documented and corroborated story is that Dahomey was so intent on making war upon my ancestors, capturing and selling them to the Europeans, that they reduced their population of male soldiers and had to rely on their women to guard their country and their (male) king. They won't tell you that Dahomey rulers sold hundreds of thousands of our BLACK Ancestors from neighboring tribes and nations to the colonizing European slave traders. They won't tell you that after the British government outlawed slave trading in 1849, the BLACK Dahomey King petitioned the British government, asking to continue trading in BLACK SLAVES.[9]

These Majority Feminist fantasy movie producers are telling a distorted historical account of the brave women warriors of Dahomey. What's most important here is that of all the many positive and wonderful African stories available to be told, "WOKE Hollywood" chose to reshape history in a way that creates further disunity between the men and women of the African diaspora. No thanks, Hollywood; I'll pass on this movie. If you follow social media, you will see that many members of the Black community actively boycotted the movie. I don't need your revisionist history. I don't need your WOKE propaganda. I will do my own research and come to my own conclusions without Hollywood's propaganda. Hollywood has no **Black Values that matter** to me.

Speaking of division, back in the 90's I studied the Moynihan Report. In 1965, Senator Daniel Patrick Moynihan, in his attempt to combat the implementation of President Lyndon Baines Johnson's "Great Society" programs, commissioned a report entitled , "The Negro Family: The Case For National Action"[10]. In this report, Senator Moynihan, who served as US Assistant Secretary of Labor at the time, laid out his scholarly case against what he saw as the coming evils that would result from Johnson's Great Society programs.

Taking into account that Johnson was a well-known racist, his "Great Society" served to divide the Black American family. It separated Black men and women by replacing Black fathers with "the government", which he knew would encourage future generations of Black American women to no longer partner with Black men in order to raise families. Johnson's Great Society programs attacked and damaged the Black nuclear family. I believe the attack was intentional.

CHAPTER 2

The report broke down the basics of Johnson's attempt to take away the self-sufficiency of the Black family. Johnson's Great Society programs painted Black people, especially urban Black people, as undisciplined "savages" who were a liability to the nation and unable to survive and prosper without government intervention. Johnson was trying to institutionalize "The Subtle Bigotry of Low Expectations".

The Moynihan Report quotes the famous author, William Faulkner, in saying,"there is no such thing as equality per se, but only equality to: equal right and opportunity to make the best one can of one's life within one's capability, without fear of injustice or oppression or threat of violence". In other words, Americans have the right to "the pursuit of happiness". The government's job is not to force equality upon its citizens…only to provide conditions that are equal so individuals can make the best of their respective circumstances.

Instead, the racist Mr. Johnson instituted a devious and divisive system with which government funds would be used to create a permanent, generational underclass of mostly Black families whom he knew would soon become dependent on government assistance, and never leave it.

Every Black person I know has a relative who is part of that permanent underclass that Lyndon Johnson's Great Society programs were intended to create. Instead of a helping hand, Johnson intended to give poor Blacks a crutch that they would never stop using…a mental prison of dependency of our own making.

The Great Society programs were implemented in 1965, around the time that I was born. As a child, I remember hearing of the

"Free Money" that the government was giving out. Decades later, I can attest that most of the families I know who stooped to take those government handouts are collectively still poor. I can tell you of women who took money from "the government" who are now the great grandmothers of generations of unruly broods of children who are separated from their fathers. Back in Moynihan's day, he complained, "Almost one-fourth of non-White families are headed by a woman." Today, roughly three-fourths of Black American children are born without the presence of their fathers. You will also find that most of our prison population grew up fatherless. Most of the negative social statistics that plague the Black American community are due to the lack of fathers in Black American households. All that is courtesy of Lyndon Baines Johnson and his merry band of Ivy League social engineers.

It's rumored that Johnson once said, "If you give me what I ask for, I'll have those Niggers Voting Democrat for the next 200 years." Our nefarious president's Great Society programs encouraged Blacks to become dependent upon the government, and as a result, removed much of our collective dignity.

The following quote comes from page 155 of historian Doris Kearns Goodwin's LBJ biography. Johnson's words were spoken to Georgia's Democrat Senator, Richard Russell;

> *"These Negroes, they're getting pretty uppity these days and that's a problem for us since they've got something now they never had before, the political pull to back up their uppityness. Now we've got to do something about this, we've got to give them a little something, just enough to quiet them down, not enough to make a difference".[11]*

President Lyndon Baines Johnson succeeded in putting together systems that would damage the Black American community for generations to come. He could not have hurt Black Americans more if he had invaded the Black community with the federalized National Guard. **Black Values Mattered Not** to Lyndon Baines Johnson. He was a terrible man who I hope is getting his just desserts in hell. Perhaps one day, America's generational poor will understand that the government will only give you enough money to die on.

Whether it's Woke Hollywood's, "Woman King", or BET and it's not so subtle subversion of Black American culture, or Lyndon Johnson and his toxic Great Society programs, understand that the Black Community and specifically, the Black nuclear family, is under attack. We are losing a culture war that this country can't afford to lose. Until all Americans can feel safe and prosperous walking the streets of West Baltimore at night; until the University of Maryland's STEM programs are filled with recent graduates of Baltimore City Schools; until more Black American men and women stay married and raise families together than become divorced, we have a whole lot of work to do. Until **Black Values Matter** to the woke leftists who are creating a false racial division, America will continue to suffer.

Has Feminism Helped "The Struggle"?

Speaking of dividing families, there is a huge chasm between Black men and Black women in America. I know of no other ethnic group that allows itself to be divided the way Blacks are in modern America. What other ethnic group makes movies that show images of women mercilessly killing their men in physical combat

(The Woman King)? Is this a Black Woman's fantasy or a Majority Feminist, Marxist fantasy? Who benefits most from promoting this revisionist history? Trust me, "it ain't Black Women."

I admittedly am a traditionalist when it comes to gender; however, I have no issues with any woman who is willing to compete and win on a level playing field. In my mind, the Majority Feminist movement has hijacked the Black struggle, leading many Black women away from the traditional family structure; away from their Black men toward lives of misery, anger and loneliness. All the while, the Majority Feminist, the typical Hillary Clinton-esque northern White liberals that Martin Luther King warned us about, can count on her background and resources to ensure that she will be "OK" at the end of the day.

> *"The Negro's great stumbling block in his stride toward freedom is not the Majority Citizens Counselor or the Ku Klux Klanner, but the White moderate, who is more devoted to order than to justice". (MLK)*[12]

The "White Moderate" has clandestinely separated the Black family. Some Black women have not only allowed it, but encouraged it. What is a problem for the Black Feminist is often not a problem for the Majority Feminist. The Majority Feminist has resources that the Black Feminist usually does not have. The LGBTQ Agenda Is Not The Black Agenda. [13] Majority women from elite liberal universities have little in common with America's Black women. Liberal Majority women have co-opted the Black struggle for their own purposes…and Black women have allowed them to do so. As an example, I recommend you check out comedian Bill Burr's take on how liberal White women have, "somehow stuck themselves in the front of the line" when it comes to social issues.

He goes on to infer that the same liberal, woke women are the greatest beneficiaries of our societal system, yet "they are always bitching". [14] Perhaps the whiny, woke White women are the real problem in our society?

BTW, Hillary Clinton's mentor, Planned Parenthood's Eugenicist Founder Margaret Sanger [15] reportedly once referred to Black Americans as "Human Weeds". Black people are killing our own babies in the name of Feminism. Black Americans are roughly 13% of the US population. Blacks long since were overcome by Hispanics (19%)[16] as the second most populous ethnic group in the US. The Hispanic population is growing. The Black population is not. Let that sink in.

As such, I am for whatever supports the traditional nuclear family, especially the Black Nuclear Family. Conservative Americans in both major political parties support the American family. I do, too. So, again, has Feminism helped "The Struggle"? **Is Feminism a Black Value?** Since we are on a related subject, **Has Black Lives Matter (BLM) helped the American Black community? Does Black Lives Matter support the Black nuclear family?** Didn't they raise tens of millions of dollars from Corporate America to support the cause of inner-city Blacks? How did the greater Black community benefit from that money? Is Black America being played again? Perhaps we will address BLM in my next book?

Squeegee Boys - Menace Or Blessing?

Speaking of Baltimore, earlier in this book, I mentioned the plight of the Squeegee Boys. The media is using these young men to, once again, paint Black America in a negative light. It's terrible that these young, mostly men, are out in the street harassing commuters for money. If able-bodied young Americans can't find suitable work, our capitalist system needs a "vector check". However, here is another angle from which to view this problem.

Mayor Scott's administration has set up a pilot program where people are being paid not to work. Some folks call it Universal Basic Income. Some call it Baltimore's Guaranteed Income Pilot.[17] Some call it "slavery". The idea is that the city would pay these kids roughly $1000 per month per person to stay off the streets and not work at all, including squeegee work. So, instead of encouraging job growth, as he promised during his campaign, Mayor Scott is offering dependence upon the government. From what I can see, the Squeegee Boys have mostly rejected his offer…and rightfully so. Mayor Scott's handout creates more reliance upon the government.

Although I don't approve of the Squeegee Boys extortionist tactics, I applaud them for refusing to accept the government's attempt at bribery. In their own way, they are acting as entrepreneurs, boldly taking their fates into their own hands. Some folks might see their hustle as the American Spirit in action. From my frequent trips into Baltimore, I see that Mayor Scott's attempt to bribe the Squeegee Boys isn't working. The Squeegee Boys are alive and well, defiantly resisting the government's veiled Marxist attempt to implement Universal Basic Income.

Chapter 3
POLITICS, CHURCHES AND BIG MONEY

How Can Black People Lead America In Both Church Attendance And Negative Social Statistics?

I sometimes wonder why things are the way they are. Black Americans still lead our nation in negative social statistics.[18] It's been that way for decades and will probably continue to be that way.

The US Bureau of Justice Statistics estimates that in 2008, there were more than 846,000 black men in prison, making up 40.2% of all inmates in the system. Of all Black American men that were born in 1965 or later, with less than a high school diploma, 60% have a prison record.[19] (Michelle Alexander – HuffPost).

Black Americans make up roughly 13% of the US population, but we make up almost 40% of the prison population. WTF? As parents, as leaders, as role models, what are we doing so wrong that so many of our Black men spend time in prison? There are over three-thousand churches in Baltimore. Can't they stop this madness? What are we doing wrong? What are we doing right? And of those things that we are doing right, why does the media not tell our story?

Churches Got COVID (PPP) Money. Where Is It?

I survived COVID-19. I got it in January 2022. I chose to not be vaccinated, relying on my faith and my good health. Even though I was hospitalized for seven days at a cost of twenty-six thousand dollars, I did not die. A whole lot of people got COVID-19 and did not die. I felt well enough to come home after receiving intravenous fluids and one day of hospitalization (incarceration), yet they kept me in the hospital against my will for six more days. They gave me the experimental drug, "Remdesivir"[20] without my approval, while I slept.

I am not an "anti-vaxxer". Having retired from serving my country after more than two decades of periodic overseas deployments, I have taken more shots than most Americans. I felt differently about the COVID-19 vaccine. Perhaps I will discuss my reasoning at another time. For now, I will say that I was disappointed in the performance of our government during COVID-19, and I was especially disappointed in the performance of our religious establishment as a whole. The right to decide what goes into one's own body is a fundamental natural law, as far as I am concerned (My Body, My Choice). I understand that our country was faced with an unprecedented viral threat of dubious origin, might I add. In 2020, we didn't know what to make of COVID-19, nor how we should respond to it.

The government's response was "to try" to force all citizens to take their hastily prepared vaccine. At the time, I was a civil servant. I was told that I had to take the vaccine to keep my job. After my religious waver was denied, I refused the vaccine. My refusal was part of my decision calculus to leave the Federal government after thirteen years.

CHAPTER 3

Many of my military and government peers also refused the vaccine. One was a Coast Guard Chief Petty Officer who was sixteen years into her career. The Coast Guard tried to force her to take the government's unproven vaccine while she was pregnant. I applaud her and her Coast Guard Petty Officer husband for refusing to take the vaccine. Risking the health of their unborn child was too much of a price to pay. I'd like to think that I would be as courageous under the same circumstances.

Of the many things that disappointed me about our nation's response to COVID-19 was the response of our religious establishments. Our churches, synagogues, mosques and such are supposed to be places where the faithful gather to gain strength and courage in times of adversity. Instead, I witnessed most of our religious leaders conceding to the demands of our government with no concern for the hard-won rights of citizens. Most churches did everything in their power to keep citizens separated and devoid of power. I understood the need to slow the spread of infection, but I also understood our government's responsibility to protect citizen's rights and desires. Most healthy people under the age of 60 were at very little risk from COVID-19. Our government knew this, but pressed on with their plan. Now that the pandemic is over (according to Joe Biden)[21], many of those same citizens are suffering from all manner of mental setbacks (fear, suicide, and odd physical maladies like myocarditis, heart attacks, etc.) that I believe came from bad decisions made by our government and our religious community. Being that this country was founded from the desire of a few European immigrants who were willing to fight for the freedom to worship as they saw fit, it's odd that our churches, for the most part, looked away as the government trampled our individual liberties during the COVID-19 pandemic.

As it turns out, things were not quite as they seemed. A Newsweek article, dated July 7, 2020, says "Religious Organizations Receive $7.3 Billion in Paycheck Protection Program (PPP) Loans, Megachurches Amass Millions".[22] Could it be that our government bought the silence and complicity of our faith communities? Could it be that our churches were bought and paid for? Could it be that our religious systems failed us when we needed them the most?

The government encouraged people to shelter in place, work from home, etc. Most churches encouraged people to "take the jab". I understand why people were afraid. They should have been. In Maryland, our places of worship were forced to shut down at the request of the government. Churches collected huge sums of virtually free money from the government, while church goers were slowly losing their faith. Many churches just counted their cash while their congregations faced the dreaded COVID-19, separate and alone. I understand that many people were scared and wanted to take the vaccines, but from my perspective, healthy people under sixty had very little risk of death from COVID-19. There was no reason to scare the majority of the world's population. There was no reason to bankrupt America and the Western world.

The Multi-Cultural church that I attended went "hook, line and sinker" into the Federal COVID-19 response. They shut down church services when the congregation's spiritual needs were at the greatest that I have ever seen. In the meantime, I continued to work for the Department of Defense (DoD) as an "emergency essential employee" from the beginning of COVID-19 in March 2020 to when I retired from the government in January 2022. My emergency essential status prohibited me from teleworking for the most of the pandemic. The churches that I saw did not serve the people. They served themselves.

Their response to COVID-19 was similar to their response to the problems of the City of Baltimore. There are reportedly six thousand churches in Baltimore. Most claim to be places of faith, but the results of their faith seems to be only surface level. Churchmen and laypeople appear to be righteous and pious, but what is the "fruit of their labor"? More crime, more violence and more opportunities to dress up in our Sunday best and look down upon those who don't believe as we do?

What's worse, it appears that the Black churches were a big target of the mass vaccination program? It's well known that the government has used the Black American community as unknowing lab experiments on more than one occasion (e.g., The Tuskegee Experiment, Henrietta Lacks,[23] etc), but somehow, many in the Black community readily took the government's vaccines with little scrutiny. The collective Black Church led its people right into taking this untested, irreversible "gene therapy". To me, that makes zero sense. I decided to take my chances with my own God-given immunity. Working on the inside of the government for thirty-four years, I developed a healthy suspicion of it. Like President Reagan, I believe in "Trust, But Verify. To me, trust in an institution that has repeatedly demonstrated that **Black Values Don't Matter to it** is a risk that I am not willing to take.

The truth will come out eventually, but the following statistics concerning "All-Cause Mortality" give me pause. This recent quote from the National Institutes Of Health sums up my concerns:

> *"The impact of the COVID-19 pandemic on all-cause mortality was considerably greater than that indicated by official counts of victims. Limited testing capacity and causes of death*

other than COVID-19 could have contributed to the increase in overall mortality rates."[24]

I interpret these words from the NIH as government-speak for people are not dying **"FROM** COVID-19. They are dying **"WITH** COVID-19". To me, those words are code for, "COVID-19 is causing other diseases that kill people.

On 19 Sept 22, Joe Biden said that "COVID-19 Is Over". [25] Personally, I don't think that we have seen the last of COVID. There is too much money to be made and too many agenda's to be fulfilled. As the great Winston Churchill once said, "Never let a good crisis go to waste".

Is Drag Queen Story Time Good For Our Children?

Why do parents expose their children to Drag Queen Story Time? In case you are unaware, it has become popular among "woke" parents to bring their children to see grown men dress up like women and gyrate sexually like female strippers. I find it reprehensible that any minor should be exposed to sexualized adult entertainment. In my world, among normal, straight people, overt sexual behavior should be kept from children. But among the progressive class in today's "new America", it has become acceptable for parents to take their children to burlesque shows where men and transgender people dance around in a sexually suggestive manner.

Many of these "Drag Shows" are being held at public libraries and even military bases. The LGBTQ Lifestyle is being pushed upon our nation's families. This can't be good. Here is something to consider. One author asks the question:

CHAPTER 3

'If blackface is wrong' — imitating a Black American – 'then why is drag okay?' In other words, you're teaching these young children—you have these gaudy men who are in this caricature, this stereotypical ugly caricature mocking women—and you're teaching that to children."[26]

As parents of two successful children, my wife and I worked hard to defend our kids from premature exposure to sexualized situations. My wife and I monitored their TV viewing, their exposure to strangers, their friends and everything else we could in order to keep them from things that their innocent minds were not ready for. But some people have no problem allowing their impressionable children to be exposed to "men who dress as women".

If drag queens want to parade around in women's clothing, they should do so…in private, among willing adults. But why do they need to parade themselves around in front of innocent, impressionable children? Some of them say that they are "fighting for their rights". To that I say, the only thing these drag queens are fighting for is preferential treatment. Why do some people feel that it's acceptable to expose children to abnormal behavior such as that? Kids under the age of puberty are not thinking of sexual things. At that age, I wasn't thinking that way, and neither were my children as they grew up. Neither are any kids that I know today. Kids just want to feel love, safety, and normality.

I often wonder about these progressive parents who are willing to expose their precious children to the ugliness of men parading around dressed as women. How would they feel about exposure to female strippers, provocatively dressed and gyrating in front of their precious children? I believe the they would call the police and demand prosecution of anyone involved. So why is it OK for men to dress provocatively and gyrate suggestively in front of children, but not real women?

When I was in the military, we were expected to refrain from outwardly public sexual behavior. That was the American Way just a generation ago. I ask, "What happened to us?" Are we afraid to protect and defend our families from evil? Do **American Values Matter** anymore? How is this cultural "Assault of the LGBTQ People" affecting the Black American community? Why are churches not fighting this destructive trend? I don't know what is going on within our culture, but I believe that our Western way of life will be negatively affected unless we make changes soon.

So, is drag queen story time good for our Black American children?

What Have They Done For You Lately?

Baltimore has had a decades long string of liberal Democrat Mayors. Baltimore's last Republican mayor was Theodore McKelden, who left office in 1967. I was two years old in 1967. Below is a list of Baltimore Mayors and their signature accomplishments since 1967:

1. William D. Schaefer
2. Clarence H. Burns
3. Thomas D'Alesandro III, (Nancy Pelosi's Brother/Enough Said)
4. Kurt Schmoke
5. Martin O'Malley (Rain Tax)
6. Sheila Dixon (Left Under Questionable Circumstances)
7. Stephanie Rawlings-Blake (Did Not Seek Re-Election After The Freddie Gray Riots)

8. Catherine Pugh (Served Three Years In Prison After A Political Scandal During Her Term In Office)
9. Jack Young
10. Brandon Scott (Incumbent)

I am certain that all these folks had good intentions and worked hard during their administrations. But the cumulative result of their efforts over the past fifty-five years is that parts of Baltimore are unlivable. Crime, urban blight, drugs, etc., have residents leaving Baltimore in droves.

Baltimore has many positive traits. But despite those positive traits, it has a high cost of living, high taxes, crumbling infrastructure, poor public schools, a high crime rate and other negatives that make the city a place many citizens want to leave.

In my humble opinion, the fact that Baltimore's politics have been run by liberals since 1967 is a big factor in why businesses don't want to operate there. Baltimore goes lacking in job creation. Without good jobs, the city will continue to crumble.

Brandon Scott's 2020 Campaign Promises [27] (his words with my analysis);

- Building public safety (FAIL)
- Holistic, proven strategy to fight violence (FAIL)
- Get repeat offenders off the streets (FAIL)
- Implementing a group violence reduction strategy (FAIL)
- Stopping the flow of illegal guns (FAIL)
- Addressing the root causes of crime (FAIL)
- Transparency and Accountability: Restoring Trust in City Government (FAIL)

- In recent years, two mayors have resigned following revelations of criminal conduct while in office (FAIL)
- I will introduce concrete and measurable initiatives aimed at restoring faith between the city and its leaders (FAIL)
- Supporting Baltimore After COVID-19 (FAIL)
- Cultivating an Inclusive, Equitable Economy (FAIL)

Alarms.org lists Baltimore as the 7th most dangerous city in America.[28] Forbes Magazine lists Baltimore as #5 on its list of 10 most dangerous cities in the US in a Feb 2022 article.[29] If we judge Mayor Scott's performance by crime, Mr. Scott is failing miserably, but he is not alone. He represents the Democrat Party, and the Democrat Party is associated with failure when it comes to leading America's big cities. What is most disappointing is that Black people continue to vote as if they believe these lies and failures of the Democrat Party in the big cities? So, are these "Black Lies", Damn Lies, or both? Will we continue to ignore the long track record of poor governance in Baltimore and in most of America's big cities? Are we happy with the performance of the party we trust to govern us?

Why Do We Tolerate Poor Governance?

As I read the news, both national and local, I see where there are recent public works problems in Baltimore, Flint Michigan and Jackson Mississippi. In these cases, people can't drink city water. It's contaminated with lead, E.Coli or whatever. In the case of Flint MI, years ago President Obama went there and sipped the water to verify it was "OK" to drink. I watched the video. From what I saw, there is no guarantee that the water the President drank came from Flint's water system. As I remember, that happened in 2016 during Mr. Obama's Presidency. As I watched the YouTube video from that event, I saw President Obama giving a speech on how safe the water was. Michael Moore did a documentary on it. "The Democrats apparently aren't the party that is gonna come to the rescue" (Michael Moore, Fahrenheit 9/11) [30]. Mr. Moore apparently is not convinced that the water was OK to drink. Aren't both he and President Obama prominent, nationally known Democrats, sworn to ideologically support each other?

Recently, in Jackson Mississippi, the same problem happened again. Their water is undrinkable. Residents can't bathe in it or even brush their teeth or cook. As of 6 Sept, the problem had not been solved. The city is "80% Black", according to a report from Reuters.

The Honorable Chokwe Antar Lumumba was elected Mayor of Jackson Mississippi in 2017.[31] He has a degree in sports entertainment law. Mayor Lumumba has a significant background in the church community. His father was once the mayor of Jackson, so politics appears to be in his blood. He is a community organizer and the "youngest mayor in Jackson's History". But what has he accomplished in his young life of thirty-four years? We know that he is Black. We know that he is a Democrat. Has he run a successful business? Has he had a successful career in anything other than politics? Is he ready to fix Jackson's problems other than just complain about them? From where does he receive his funding?

In August 2022, the Baltimore Sun reported that the city's water was "undrinkable, contaminated with E.Coli bacteria". There is a boiled water advisory. "Guidance from the city is limited", minus a boiled water alert for the area where most of the city's Black population lives.

Mayor Brandon Scott, mentioned previously, appears to be some sort of community organizer. What has he accomplished in is young life of thirty-two years? We know that he is Black. We know that he is a Democrat. Has he raised a successful family? Has he run a successful business? Has he had a successful career in anything other than politics? From where does he receive his funding?

Karen Weaver served as Flint Michigan's mayor during the beginning of its water crisis. After this crisis happened on her watch, the citizens of Flint voted her out. Fast forward a few years, and she is (as of this writing) running for office again. Having failed the city of Flynt during its water crisis, as of Sept 2022, she is the leading challenger to the current mayor. From what I can see of her resume, she is a psychologist. The current mayor, Sheldon Neeley, is a trained engineer. That is good. Hopefully, he has the technical know-how and leadership ability to help fix Flint's water system. I wish him well. However, why is Karen Weaver running again after she failed to secure Flint's water system in her first term as mayor? Who supports her? Could it be that the mostly Black female electorate is voting for her because she looks like them? There is an old saying that lends itself to this situation, "You get what you pay for." With reference to her dismal failure as mayor in her first term, what would make citizens think that she might do better in a second term?

That is a real issue. Crumbling infrastructure is only one of the myriad of problems facing our country's urban populations. Each city has its own specific set of problems that needs to be addressed. I recommend that the electorates of the respective municipalities make the primary criteria for election, the demonstrated ability to solve problems…not just ethnicity or skin color. Otherwise, these municipalities will end up with a string of failed mayors and a mounting list of problems. Baltimore, Flint Michigan, Jackson Mississippi, etc., have something in common. That commonality is that their citizens elect leaders based on "skin color" and ethnicity as opposed to the candidate's track record. Isn't selecting a candidate based on their looks as opposed to their qualifications an example of "Racism"?

By the way, our Federal government is not without blame. How, in good conscience, can our President send tens of billions of dollars to make war on other countries while America's inner cities crumble and loyal citizens who voted for him suffer? Perhaps the votes of Black Americans are sold too cheaply?

Furthermore, Democrats are not the only party with leadership problems. If Baby George Bush and Dick "Darth Vader" Cheney had been more interested in protecting Americans rather than war-profiteering in the Middle East, we wouldn't be having this conversation.

Let's apply this model across the board to the many problems facing urban populations like Baltimore: crime, education, jobs, healthcare…etc. Americans should seek out and elect only the most successful and qualified candidates for high office. I understand people's desire to elect people who "look like them", but I also understand that Americans need to put forth their best efforts in an attempt to keep our country free, safe and livable. Believe it or not, "Just because someone has your skin, don't make them kin." If Americans want better results, they must elect the most qualified and objective candidates, regardless of ethnicity or gender. If that person is Black, so be it. If not, ethnicity and gender should be less of a factor. Black folks have "played sucker" to the Democrat party for decades. It's been a long time since the Democrat party "earned"

Black votes. Until we can all stroll through West Baltimore after dark without fear, then we still have work to do.

Why Do We Tolerate Poor Leaders?

In a Baltimore Sun article dated May 2016, the Reverend Jamal Bryant addressed concerns that he fathered a child out of wedlock, and he talked about his recent divorce.[32] At the time, he was firmly entrenched at Baltimore's "Empowerment Temple," where he served as a long-time pastor. As of Sept 2022, Mr. Bryant is pastoring a Mega church in the Atlanta area.

Pastor Bryant and his ex-wife divorced seven years into their marriage in 2008 after his infidelity was discovered. So what happened after Bryant departed? He was hired to replace accused pedophile pastor, Eddie Long, who has an even more extensive history as an infamous, self-serving charlatan.

A quick internet search on "Pastor Bryant" reveals the following headlines;

- Jamal Bryant Denounces Domestic Violence After James Fortune Pleads Guilty To Assaulting Wife.
- His Mistress Had A Paternity Test Completed In Order To Confirm The Paternity Of His Illegitimate Child.
- His Lawyers Advised Him To "Not Share Any Details With The Public".
- Jamal Bryant Tax Lien Troubles From Baltimore.

Information on deceased Pastor Eddie Long of Atlanta's New Birth Missionary Church, where Bryant now pastors, can be found by a simple internet search. During my quick review, I found the following; "In the Fox interview, a vehement Parris (Long's victim) said, "Long manipulated us from childhood" under the guise of providing a fatherly influence".[33]

> *Christianity's holy book says, "For a bishop must be blameless, as the steward of God; not self-willed, not soon angry, not given to wine, no striker, not given to filthy lucre".[34]*

Last I checked, both Jamal Bryant and Eddie Long, before him, claimed to be bishops. No wonder so many Blacks fail to prosper, when they choose this kind of man [or woman] as their leader. Furthermore, Matthew 23:8-10 KJVS says,

> **"But be not ye called Rabbi**: *for one is your Master, even Christ; and all ye are brethren. And call no man your father upon the earth: for one is your Father, which is in heaven. Neither be ye called masters: for one is your Master, even Christ.[35]*

So let me get this straight…our own King James Bible states clearly that we are not to call a man "Master, Father, Reverend, Rabbi, Pastor, or any such title"? This passage says that we are all "brethren". But the Church thrives on hierarchical titles; Elder, Deacon, Mother of the Church? How can we get along without the pyramidal, overlord-based structure that we were taught by our slave masters?

Whether or not these "pastors" did the heinous deeds they are accused of is not my focus. My question is, why do Black Americans continue to follow flawed leaders? Is there something inherently wrong with us?

My intention is to bring to light the fact that Blacks follow and support these charlatans no matter how many times they fail their followers. Black people will follow these men [and women] even when they are accused of pedophilia, as was the case with Eddie Long. I thought that pastors were expected to be chaste, good hearted paragons of virtue? How can Black people continue to follow leaders who demonstrate this kind of failure and expect to prosper? The last time I checked, there were more than six-thousand churches within the city limits of Baltimore. With all these pastors, deacons, elders, lay-people and flock involved in so very many churches, why has Baltimore become a place where so many people no longer want to live?

Here is yet another bible verse that I was not taught in church. I discovered this as an adult while studying the bible on my own.

> *"But the anointing which ye have received of him abideth in you,* **and ye need not that any man teach you***: but as the same anointing teacheth you of all things, and is truth, and is no lie, and even as it hath taught you, ye shall abide in him".* 1 John 2:27 KJVS [36]

Is this passage saying that we don't need a preacher? …that we can get what we need spiritually from the holy spirit, who anoints us from within ourselves? Amazing!

Since we're on the subject, here is a yet another scripture that resonates with me. I wonder if it resonates with you?

> *"Servants, be obedient to them that are your masters according to the flesh, with fear and trembling, in singleness of your heart, as unto Christ";* [37] *Ephesians 6:5 KJVS*

Are we supposed to treat our bosses or slave masters like Christ? I serve no earthly master. My ancestors paid a steep price so I wouldn't have to be a slave. Anyone who tries to enslave me or anyone I know will regret the day that they tried. With all the revisions written into the bible over the last millennia, I wonder why this passage is still there? They removed the entire book of Enoch and several other books of the Apocrypha, but this passage remains? I am not one to question the Bible, but this passage seems "manipulated". Could it be that all this "leadership" that we get from clergy is unneeded? Could it be that all this authority that we vest in organized religion is not necessary. Could it be that all this money we give to churches, including tax-free 501(c)(3) status is not necessarily the right thing to do? Could it all be a SCAM? I question EVERYTHING.

Here is my theory. The psyche of Black Americans has been damaged by the ugliness of the "Middle Passage" and of "Slavery". As such, our ethnic group has been taught to be overly tolerant of its leaders…to expect less of them…to be protective of them…even when they are clearly wrong. Should we sacrifice our values for the sake of following flawed leaders? Should we not hold our leaders to high standards? Perhaps if we held our leaders to a higher standard, we might not have to ask the question, **"Do Black Values Matter?"**

Would Republicans Be Any Better?

Recently, I was in the barber's chair. I love going to the barbershop. There, I can shoot the breeze with the fellas and relax. There are no subjects that are off limits and sometimes things even get a little heated. My Black barber, "Mike", has been cutting my hair for about two years now. I have a standing appointment every two weeks, no matter what. As he cuts my hair, any subject might come up.

As we chatted, the sports commentator, Shannon Sharpe, was enraged in a way that I have never seen him. I have followed Shannon and his brother Sterling throughout their careers as we are from the same part of the country and roughly similar in age. I always root for them to do well. So, why was Shannon Sharpe as mad at Brett Favre as I have seen him with anyone?

Bret Favre[38] was reportedly found to be involved in a scam to use Federal welfare funds to divert $5M to buy a new volleyball court for his alma mater, the University of Southern Mississippi. The scam involved big money donors from Big Pharma, a former Mississippi Governor and the eventual misappropriation of over $70M in public funds meant to aid some of the poorest people in our country.

Like I am for the Sharpe brothers, I was a huge Brett Favre fan. He is an NFL Hall-of-Famer, and until this incident, a reportedly good guy. He is also supposedly an evangelical Christian and an avid Trump supporter. This man surely has made well past $100M in his career, to include lucrative endorsement deals with several companies. With all these blessings, he chooses to steal from the poorest of the poor to build a new volley ball court for his college volleyball playing daughter? He did so while thousands of his fellow Mississippians in Jackson have no clean water to drink.

What are we to make of this situation in relation to the water crisis in Jackson, the water crisis in Baltimore and the countless episodes of government corruption and mismanagement that seems to plague our nation right now? What are we to make of the apparent crisis in conscience that we are suffering from? Party affiliation seems to matter more than our personal character, as human beings. At this point, I just don't know what to think. I guess **Black Values Don't Matter** to rich athletes like Brett Favre.

What Did President Obama Give Us For Our Votes?

I was living in Texas and still in the military when I first heard of Barack Obama. Honestly, I paid little attention to him. He was a relatively new senator from Illinois. He was Black and progressive. That's nice, I thought to myself as I completed the last tour of my military career. I noticed the effect he had on my wife and the other Blacks I knew.

The Black community was starved for legitimate leadership, with Jesse Jackson and Al Sharpton at the height of their respective political powers. To me, these two guys were political hucksters, always looking for the next "race hustle" that would raise their profile and add to their coffers.

Mr. Obama appeared to be different from Jackson, Sharpton and their ilk. He was a smooth, handsome, Ivy League lawyer. He was a family man, married to another Ivy League lawyer. At first, I thought, who would vote for man named "Barack Husain Obama" while our country was in the middle of an overseas war against Muslim nations. Again, my wife and other Blacks had a curious and building reaction towards him. It was almost as if he was some sort of "messiah".

At the time, our president was Baby George "Dubya" Bush…the 2nd American President from the Bush family. Bush and his Vice

President, Dick Cheney (i.e., Darth Vader), started the disastrous wars in Iraq and Afghanistan, supposedly chasing weapons of mass destruction or terrorists who had nothing to do with the 9/11 attacks on this country. By 2008, Bush was highly unpopular due to his many failed policy outcomes. He allowed Dick Cheney and Donald Rumsfeld to mine money from the pursuit of unneeded war and mayhem across the planet.

With these jokers in office, Obama offered a breath of fresh air. He was cool, smart, handsome, engaging, young and "not White". As he was being pushed as a viable presidential candidate, more and more people jumped on his band wagon. In 2008, as I retired from the military, I wanted to learn more about national politics and I wanted to help him get elected. I went to a rally in support of his presidential primary campaign in Texas. Well, I opened my big mouth, one thing led to another, and I found myself selected to be the precinct chairman for his campaign in my North San Antonio neighborhood.

I had no idea what I was doing, but somehow, I fit the part and people put me in place as the face of the campaign in my neighborhood. Fresh out of the military, I was a true rookie.

Regardless of my support for Obama, what I was mostly concerned with was Hillary Clinton and her crew. I despised Clinton, her husband and her whole condescending ideology. To me, she was what was wrong with our country. She was that third-grade teacher who sized me up from the beginning, assuming my future wouldn't amount to much. She was that patronizing, privileged "Karen" who would always see me and all minorities through "the soft bigotry of low expectations". I despised her, her elitist daughter, and her rapey-assed ex-President husband. Even though Bill was from Arkansas, the Clintons were those "Northern Liberals" that MLK warned us about. They were the ones who prefer "Order Over Justice". So yes, I wanted to get involved, and Obama's campaign seemed to be a great fit for me to cut my teeth. Opposing the Clinton campaign was the perfect way to do that. What's more unusual is that I was a "registered Republican" while I was doing all this work for Obama. Texas is one of the few states that cares less about party affiliations. So yes, I was chairman of Mr. Obama's North San Antonio area primary campaign, while being a good old, dyed-in-the-wool Republican. Ain't that something? (I Love Texas)

As it turns out, Obama lost Texas, but he won the Presidency. Gone were Bush, Cheney, Rumsfeld and their miserable, neo-conservative, war-mongering crew. Also, Hillary Clinton would not be elected President. I considered that to be a victory for humanity. I guess I could get used to this Obama fellow. At least he was half-Black. At least he had some understanding of my struggles. At least he understood Black America. Well, I don't know if any of that is quite true.

Mr. Obama is not the "Son of Slaves" like me. His father was Kenyan. His mother and father were Marxist-leaning university professors. His mom was a bit of a hippy. His Marxist-leaning father abandoned their family as Obama grew up in Hawaii.

Obama's effect on the Black American community was profound. As I said before, he was a messiah-like figure. People who had been turned off of politics for years were now suddenly turned on. Black racial pride swelled as he campaigned across the country, spreading his message of hope and change. I, too, was a fan. The Republicans nominated John McCain as Obama's 2008 opponent and Bain Capital's Mitt Romney in 2012. Neither could stand up to the charisma and coolness of Mr. Obama, especially not to the Black community who overwhelmingly and unquestionably supported "their President". However, what did we get out of our unwavering support of Mr. Obama?

From what I see, he did very little for the Black community. Instead, he ushered in more support for "the LGBTQ People" than he did for Black Americans. What I noticed was the elevation and normalization of gay and trans people's issues **at the expense of Black people's issues**. I saw Black people's wealth in this country diminish. Inner city Blacks in Baltimore, for example, are now living in a hell-scape of higher crime, underperforming schools and crumbling infrastructure. It's pretty much the same in all Democrat-run inner-cities across the nation. Obama may have looked somewhat like other minorities, but he showed that his loyalty lies with the "Ivy League Elites" and the one-percent, more than the Black Americans who proudly put him in office… the same one percent who he failed to prosecute after the housing market crash of 2008.

I will admit that I wanted to see some "hope and change". But what did he actually do for the Black people who supported him? He went from "community organizer" to multi-millionaire speaker, Elite 1-Percenter and corporate shill. In the Black community, even today, questioning his policies might result in a physical altercation. Damn, are we that gullible? Are we that subject to the "bait and switch" game? Are we suckers? "Fool me once, shame on you. Fool me twice, shame on me".

Let's compare what President Obama did for the Black community and what he did for the LGBTQ community?

CHAPTER 3

Specifically For Black Americans	
Awarded $1.2 Billion To Black Farmers	Specifically For Blacks
Expanded Funding For HBCUs	Specifically For Blacks
Signed The Crack Cocaine Bill (Fair Sentencing Act)	**Not** Specifically For Blacks
Passed Health Care Reform (Affordable Care Act)	**Not** Specifically For Blacks
Created The Civil Rights Division Of The Justice Department	**Not** Specifically For Blacks
He Made Black People Feel Good.	Specifically For Blacks

Specifically for LGBTQ People	
President Obama Leaves A Monumental Legacy On LGBTQ Rights	Specifically For LGBTQ People
No President In History Has Done More For Lesbian, Gay, Bisexual, Transgender And Queer Rights Than Barack Obama	Specifically For LGBTQ People
Obama Helped Lift The Ban On LGBTQ People Serving Openly In The Military	Specifically For LGBTQ People
In February 2011, Then-Attorney General Eric Holder Announced That The Administration Would Not Defend The Defense Of Marriage Act In Court.	Specifically For LGBTQ People
Obama First Made A Public Statement In Favor Of Marriage Equality On May 9, 2012.	Specifically For LGBTQ People
The Federal Government Told Public Schools They Must Allow Transgender Students To Use Bathrooms That Correspond With Their Gender Identity.	Specifically For LGBTQ People

[39]

CHAPTER 3

To me, it looks like the generously counted 5% of citizens who are LGBTQ People got a better deal than the +13% of American Citizens Of African Descent who of voted for him. Did We Get Fooled Again?

Where Are My Reparations?

A dear friend and I have a long running debate concerning "Reparations". She and her husband have done well in life, enjoying all the trappings of middle-class success. Compared to how we grew up in rural North Carolina, they have achieved the American Dream. My dear friend's line of thinking is that she is "owed" reparations for slights that were suffered by our slave ancestors. My dear friend believes that someone owes reparations to all Black American people. Many Black Americans still feel that way, while they live in million-dollar houses and drive Range Rovers.

My position is that my slave ancestors died centuries ago. Given all the pain, shame and anguish they suffered, it is my sworn duty to honor their legacy by never allowing myself or anyone I know to suffer the evils of slavery. It will be over my cold, dead body before anyone I know is ever enslaved. That is part of the reason that I stayed in the military so long. In summary, I am owed nothing but a fair chance to achieve my dreams and desires. God help anyone who stands in my way.

Since we had a "Black President" for two recent presidential terms… and it was Black Americans who voted for him almost universally, what exactly did he do to provide those reparations that he "Kind Of Implied" and Black folks "Kind Of Assumed" that he would provide us if he were elected? A February 2022 Fox News Article says;

"Former President Barack Obama blamed "the politics of White resistance and resentment" as the reason why he didn't push for financial Reparations for Black Americans during his presidency". The article goes on to say that "Obama appears to have changed his position on Reparations over the years."

He {President Obama} opposed Reparations during his 2008 Presidential campaign, arguing that "the best Reparations we can provide are good schools in the inner city and jobs for people who are unemployed." [40]

An Associated Press article from Aug 2008 records that "Obama says an apology would be appropriate but not particularly helpful in improving the lives of Black Americans. Reparations could also be a distraction, he said." [41]

So let me get this straight…Black Americans helped make this man the most politically powerful human being on the planet for eight years. His word was "LAW". His supporters expected him to secure "Reparations" for Black Americans during his two terms in office, but he somehow skipped the question of "Reparations" for the whole eight years of his Presidency? In 2008, while campaigning, he didn't support reparations, but in 2021, after his Presidency, with nothing to lose and under no pressure to perform, he now supports Reparations?

Oh, by the way, National Public Radio said in 2016 that President Obama approved $492M in Reparations for Native Americans.[42] LET THAT SINK IN. I am happy for our Native American citizens. God only knows what their ancestors suffered. However, did our Black President support Black America when it came to Reparations? Remember the old saying, "Fool Me Once, Shame

On You. Fool Me Twice, Shame On Me"? Oh damn, did Black America get fooled again? **Did Black Values Matter** when it came to getting the Reparations that Black America expected? I voted for him. WHERE ARE MY REPARATIONS?

Another thought to consider...if approved, who qualifies for reparations? Obama himself is bi-racial. But since his father is not "American" what percentage of reparations would he qualify for? Several children in my extended family are bi-racial. Who will determine their share of the reparations allotment. It is rumored that my great, great, great grandmother was White. Although my skin is the color of mahogany, would I still qualify for a share of reparations money?

The government won't give you anything that doesn't benefit the government in the long run. Instead of begging for handouts from the government, I believe our ancestors would expect their progeny to stand tall, become self-sufficient and take our rightful place in this land of liberty and prosperity, instead of begging for scraps from the tables of the elites.

Black Churches Got "What" From President Obama?

Black Churches have been a bastion of conservative thought since the beginning of this country. Black Churches support traditional marriage, traditional families and biblically focused living. Black Church goers are among the most conservative people in this country, however during his administration, President Obama supported same-sex marriage and other policies that are not Biblical. How can it be that Black churches supported President Obama almost universally, when they disagreed with him on some of his major policies?

The following article on the subject was published in 2012 in the "DC Spotlight" newspaper during the Obama Administration.[43]

> *"In May, President Barack Obama caught the nation off guard when he announced his support for same-sex marriage. But no group has had more qualms over his historic decision than the Black churches that, until now, have overwhelmingly supported the president".*

> *"Though many Black churches such as the Shiloh Baptist Church remain uninvolved in the national debate on gay marriage, most feel strongly about it—some for it, others against it. But almost all agree that Black church leaders and members will not stay home on Election Day."*

> *"We fought. We have a history of blood surrounding our vote, so we're going to vote. That doesn't mean we have to support gay marriage. We can skip that question and we can vote on every other issue on the ballot," said Evans. "In Maryland, what we are going to do is pull the lever against gay marriage and ignore President Obama. I'm not saying we're going to vote against Obama, we're saying that he does not support our stance."*

From what I can see back in 2012, President Obama conflated the Black American struggle for civil rights with the "LGBTQ People's" desire for America to recognize gay marriage. President of the National Black Church Initiative (NBCI), Reverend Anthony Evans, disagreed with both President Obama and the NAACP when he stated the following:

> *"The NAACP is wrong by categorizing that [marriage]. It is not a civil right; it is a privilege and it is sanctioned by the*

church and blessed by the church", Evans said. "[They're in the] same position the president is in—nobody appointed them to the word. There is nothing in biblical, church or modern literature as marriage equality. It has no validity, so whoever argues this, made up words and the church will have none of that." Evans believes the president is asking the church to ignore God's commandments. He said that the President's endorsement of same-sex marriage violates his Christianity, because as a Christian, he is supposed to obey the teachings of the church. "He is theologically out of bounds. We are going to have to sanction the President if he continues to go down this path", Evans said.[44]

Did President Obama Support "Black Values" Or LGBTQ Values?

In 2016, President Obama's administration threatened to withhold federal funding from my birth state of North Carolina because of North Carolina's House Bill 2 (HB2)[45] law, which "requires transgender people to use public restrooms that match the sex listed on their birth certificate rather than their gender identity".

What this all boils down to is that President Obama favored the rights of the LGBTQ People over the rights of the majority of the citizens of the State of North Carolina. Apparently, North Carolina's people weren't comfortable with biological men sharing bathrooms with its biological women. President Obama's position seems "unbiblical". What does the church say?

All this happened during Mr. Obama's Presidency. My question to you is…what great legislation did President Obama fight for that exclusively benefitted the Black American community? Personally,

I haven't seen any great legislation that he fought for that exclusively benefitted Black Americans. But he sure did fight for a series of legislation and executive orders designed to benefit the LGBTQ people.

I have no axe to grind against gays or transgenders. My niece is gay. I care for her and her partner deeply. I care not who you love or what you do in your home. But I do have an issue with LGBTQ people trying to "normalize" their lifestyles and sexuality upon straight people and children. I think it's crass and tasteless for anyone to be openly sexual in front of children. I think it's destructive for anyone to attempt to "groom" other people's children. Anyone who wants to influence kids should have their own and raise them, with all the consequences of parenthood.

Did President Obama usurp **Black Values** in order to advance the cause of the LGBTQ people? I think he did. More importantly, do **Black Values Matter** to President Obama? Apparently, LGBTQ People's Values mattered more to him.

I think Mr. Obama highjacked **Black Values** in order to advance a cause that is not for Black people. As I look at our cities, our economy, our state of being as an ethnicity, I ask if Black Americans benefitted from Mr. Obama's obsession with tying our Black Struggle to the issues of the LGBTQ People. As a result, "The Struggle" has been minimized, and even, dare I say, replaced.

African Americans, Black Americans and Jesse Jackson: What Is Our Allegiance To The Slave Catchers?

On 28 March, 1984, I was a nineteen-year-old college freshman at what was then, Pembroke State University (the present University

CHAPTER 3

of North Carolina at Pembroke). I was commuting from home, working my way through college. That day, I had a lifetime experience. I survived a devastating series of tornadoes that raged through my hometown of Red Springs, North Carolina.[46]

The town was wrecked by tornadoes. Several people died that evening. Electricity was out. Water and sewer services were shut down. Food was scarce. Roads were blocked from downed trees and live power lines were on the ground. Looting was rampant.

As a strapping 19-year-old man, I went out to help where I could, against my relative's better judgement. I went around to neighbors to check on them. For the first time, I saw what the term "in shock" meant. A neighbor's house was caved in from the tornadoes. Debris fell on one of the kids. As I walked through the shattered glass door to check on them, I saw this young child bleeding profusely from the head, just sitting there with a wild-eyed look on her face. The family of seven, ranging in age from six to roughly sixty all just sat there as if they were in a daze. No one moved until I let myself in.

Later that night, as I helped to clear roads and do whatever I felt was right, somehow, I found myself in the local trailer park where the tornadoes seemed to do their most devastating work. The metal trailers were twisted about like tin cans. I saw dead bodies for the first time beyond a funeral as the First Responders were pulling people from the trailers.

That night, I remember walking past the local Western Auto store. The building was imploded by a direct hit from the tornadoes. The building was gone, with only a few bricks left in what once were walls. The material on the shelves remained mostly unmoved by the storm. I had only heard that kind of thing could happen, but I saw it for myself. I could tell many, many more stories, but in summary, it was the worst night of my young life to that point.

After a few days of chaos, the White business owners complained to the state government about looting as people were literally walking down main street, taking what they wanted. Soon, the National Guard deployed. They came less to help people and more to restore order. They gave out clean water and food. I give them credit for that.

1984 was the year Jesse Jackson ran for President. Remember, "Run Jesse, Run"? That mumbly bastard actually made the national news with his campaign. Back in those days, Dan Rather was the CBS Evening News anchor. Townspeople knew things were bad when the great Dan Rather mentioned the tornadoes in Red Springs, North Carolina.

As an incentive for the people, Jesse Jackson was coming to Red Springs to give a speech and survey the damage to our tiny, devastated hamlet. Oh wow, our hero was coming to save us.

Well, here is my take on things. It was announced that Jesse Jackson would land by helicopter on the lawn of Red Springs Presbyterian Church…the largest Majority Church in a town full of Blacks and Native Americans. Ok, I get it. They needed a huge, treeless, flat lawn where they could land a couple of helicopters.

First comes the news helicopter from one of the big TV Stations in Raleigh. Most of the citizens in Red Springs couldn't receive that station with their antenna TVs. We watched CBS out of Florence, South Carolina, and NBC, out of Wilmington, North Carolina, not Raleigh. This was before the advent of cable TV, so that was a wasted effort. Next comes what I later recognized as a Huey from Ft Bragg. The helicopter circled and landed on the huge lawn of the most powerful, prosperous, well attended "White Folks" church in town. The wind whirled and two rotor blades eventually stopped.

Out pops the great Jesse Jackson and his entourage in all their splendor. People from all around came to see the Presidential candidate calm the nerves of the citizens who were still suffering from the tornado's devastation.

He stepped down from the helicopter and was handed a bullhorn. There he majestically stood, surrounded by a "Rainbow Coalition" of poor people, starving for a good word from "the Man".

Jesse Jackson took a breath and commenced to say what I interpreted as, "YOU NEGROS STOP LOOTING." Then he got back on his helicopter and flew away. He was on the ground for about five minutes. He didn't help move any downed trees or power lines off the roads. He didn't pass out any water or food. He didn't solve any of our problems. All I remember was "Stop Looting", "the Government is in charge" and "Vote For Me". Since then, I have despised Jesse Jackson and all that he stands for. On that spring day in 1984, **Black Values Did Not Matter** to Jesse Jackson. What mattered was "media coverage" of him looking Presidential. What mattered was him "towing the line for the elites". Thank God he lost his bid for the Presidency. That soulless shill would have been a terrible President. The country would have suffered greatly.

Speaking of Jesse Jackson, to my knowledge, he popularized the phrase "African American". I have never liked that phrase. I prefer the term, "Black American". I try to avoid the term "African

American" because I was not raised in Africa and my values don't reflect African culture. The term African American honors the very slave catchers who hunted my ancestors, imprisoned them and sold them to the European colonizers. Right, wrong or indifferent, my culture is uniquely American.

From my studies of the peoples of Africa, I find that my ancestors from Ghana were captured by the Ashanti and Dahomey tribes, jailed in slave castles and sold to the colonizers. If you doubt me, study up on the writings of Harvard Professor Henry Louis Gates.[47] He had the "beer summit" with President Obama, years ago. He makes his living as an expert in Black American history. I have followed him for decades.

I have more in common with my Jewish American neighbor than I do with a representative from an African continent with over 1500 separate languages and cultures…none of which I am very familiar.

I have never been to Africa, so why would I put "Africa" first when describing my ethnicity? The term "Black American" suits me much better, as I am culturally, an American and also culturally "Black". During my overseas travels, foreigners treated me as an American, not just a Negro. They instinctively knew that I was not African. I like American Football, American Barbecue and American Culture. **Black American Values Matter** to me. That will never change.

The Ashanti Tribe

In June of 2020, Speaker Of The House, Nancy Pelosi and long-time Congressman Jim Clyburn of South Carolina [48], bent the knee to Black Lives Matter (BLM), while wearing Kente Cloths around their necks in solidarity with BLM. What I saw from these two members of Congress was the most blatantly patronizing political stunt that I have EVER seen.

First of all, these two old codgers needed help to kneel down, and they needed help to get up. They are old…really old. And wearing those Kente Cloths, they looked really, really unworthy of office… dare I say, stupid.

As for the Kente Cloths they wore, as a Black man, I was totally offended. Pelosi occupies the same rung of disgust for me that the Clintons do, so I expect little from her in the way of understanding my culture. Clyburn is Black and should know better.

The Kente Cloth comes from West Africa's Ashanti Tribe. The Ashantis were a dominant warring tribe in West Africa, enslaving my ancestors and selling them to the European colonizers. A symbol of royalty in Ashanti society was the "Kente Cloth". So, Speaker Pelosi and Congressman Clyburn wore the favored wealth symbol of some of the original oppressors of the African diaspora. The Ashanti tribe were among the "slave catchers" in Africa, helping to capture my ancestors and put them in slave castles [49] on the West coast. That way, the Europeans didn't need to go into the African interior to secure slaves. The Europeans didn't want to expose themselves to tropical diseases and the dangers of traveling in a land where they were an easily recognized minority, known for "stealing human beings". Instead, they built slave castles where they could just sail their ships to the West African shores and buy my ancestors from the slave catchers with impunity. To me, Nancy Pelosi wearing a Kente Cloth is an insult to all people of African descent. It's "Cultural Appropriation" at its worst. Why do Black people allow Nancy Pelosi, Jim Clyburn and the Democrats to insult us like that? Thanks a lot, Nancy, you old Hag.

Why Are The Elites Bringing In So Many Refugees and Migrants?

> *"More folks, particularly black folks, need to know what's going on. It's inherently wrong to see American citizens struggle with housing and food and yet to see illegal immigrants receive furnished apartments and grocery vouchers"* — **Dr. Ray**

Afghan Refugees

I was working at the Department of Homeland Security (DHS) during my last posting for the DoD. I served as DoD's Liaison to DHS Headquarters where I interfaced routinely with the DHS Director and his staff. They were nice people who treated me well. I am still close to several of them.

In August of 2021, things turned south as Mr. Biden decided to abruptly shut down America's twenty-year-old war in Afghanistan. Mind you, I supported leaving Afghanistan, but not like this. I had been there in uniform. I knew that the DoD had plans in place to retrograde out of there in an orderly fashion. If there is one thing we do well in DoD, it's logistics.

At times, we had as many as one hundred thousand troops in Afghanistan over the course of 20 years. That is One Hundred Thousand military people plus "beans, bombs, and bullets" for all of them. That means aircraft, medical teams, intelligence people and gear. Extensive and expensive was our investment in this Afghan

CHAPTER 3

Police Action. We lost huge amounts of blood and treasure. We killed scores and scores of Afghan opponents.

For Mr. Biden to just pick up and leave in such a harried and thoughtless fashion showed a level of disrespect to all service members that I had never seen from our government before. Why we left in such a hurry at that time in history made no sense to me. We left scads of expensive war making gear over there, and we left people. As of this writing, I believe that our NATO allies had people over there for several months before they were extracted, living on the Afghan economy, yet unable to leave for fear of capture. Our American propaganda slogan of "never leaving a man behind" is only just that…"a propaganda slogan". Our soldiers and those of our allies were deemed "expendable", as our Ivy League educated leadership considered the "cost-benefit analysis" of whether to leave people behind or not. It's a sordid and dishonorable business that we have evolved into.

Our government was not prepared for the sudden influx of Afghan refugees into the United States. To complicate matters, Biden set up an almost impossible timeline for DoD to leave Afghanistan.

Back in the states, DHS was designated as "Lead Federal Agency" for the Afghan resettlement. What that means is that DHS was in charge of resettling roughly seventy-nine thousand new Afghans into America. DHS had NEVER run such a large program before. They didn't have the budget, nor the facilities, nor the expertise to do something like this well. On top of that, this country was in the middle of dealing with COVID-19, so roughly 80% of DHS's work force was "Teleworking".

As NORTHCOM's rep, I was in the middle of the action, helping to facilitate interagency coordination. I could tell you many stories about the effort, but what is relevant for this book is that the US Government spent roughly $1400 per day, per Afghan refugee, getting them culturally acclimated to living in the US, with language training, allowances for lodging, food, clothing, medical care, etc. As of 22 Aug 2022, the US had absorbed roughly seventy-nine thousand Afghan refugees with more on the way. My backwoods education says that equals $110M per day.

On 8 Sept, The Daily Wire published, "IG Report Blasts Biden's Homeland Security For Improperly Vetting Afghan Refugees".

> *Between July 2021 and January 2022, the United States welcomed more than 79,000 Afghan evacuees as part of Operation Allies Refuge (OAR)/Operation Allies Welcome (OAW). Now a report from the Office of the Inspector General (OIG) for the Department of Homeland Security (DHS) concluded the Biden administration's* **DHS *"may have admitted or paroled individuals into the United States who pose a risk to national security and the safety of local communities."*** [50]

Apparently, I wasn't the only one who had a problem with allowing unvetted refugees into our country. Up until 18 Jan 22, during my last 12 months of Federal service, one of my tasks was helping to bring refugees into the US. After 34 years, this was the job posting that made me retire from government service. This was my "line in the sand".

This is one of the many things that our government asked me to do that I hated…along with the vaxx mandates…along with exiting Afghanistan in an undignified fashion…along with starting another war in the Ukraine…along with various other dirty deeds, etc.

I don't begrudge the Afghans. Those of them who are legitimate supporters of DoD would have been killed had they stayed in Afghanistan. However, if our government can spend over $100M per day on refugees, how come we can't spend more money rescuing Baltimore and America's inner-cities where large numbers of American-born Blacks citizens live?

Haitian Refugees

Complicating matters was the Haitian Refugee Crisis.[51] During the fall of 2021, eighteen thousand Haitian migrants showed up under a bridge near the border crossing station, south of Del Rio Texas. It was a huge mass exodus of people from yet another poor country. All this was happening at literally the same time that our government was dealing with the Afghan Refugee Crisis and with all the complications of COVID-19. I found the timing to be incredibly odd. Eighteen thousand people massing in virtually the same spot on the globe, under a bridge south of a US Immigration station, all while the Federal government had its hands full with the Afghan Refugee Crisis and with all the complications of COVID-19? What are the odds against all that happening at once?

Coast Guard Aviation was called into fly some of the Haitian men back to Port-au-Prince. I was briefed that this "repatriation" didn't go well. I was told that some of the Haitian men didn't want to go back to Haiti. They expressed displeasure by physically attacking the flight crews. But that is another story for another time. In the meantime, thousands of Haitian men, women and children disappeared in to the vastness of our cities. Once again, from my post at DHS HQ, I saw our government's reaction and failures. To me "the system" was being intentionally overwhelmed…overloaded to its breaking point.

The media posted false propaganda pictures of Border Patrol agents appearing to chase and beat Haitians at the border in an attempt to "corral" them.[52] As a result, I saw parades of reporters and organizations escorted into the DHS Secretary's conference room for what appeared to be daily status briefs. Remember, at this time, a large percentage of DHS was teleworking because of the fear of contracting COVID-19.

How did all these refugees end up in the same location at the same time? There had to be some sort of coordinated effort in order to pull this off. Logistically, it was quite a feat to coordinate the movement of all these people and have them all arrive at virtually the worst possible time and place for the US Government to handle.

Oh, but there is more. Have we forgotten the US Southwest Border…the place where undocumented migrants, illegal drugs and fentanyl enter this country? The US Border has been poorly governed since Mr. Biden assumed the Presidency.[53] President Trump wasn't perfect, but his administration had a far better handle on US Border Security than the Biden Administration. I was briefed routinely that three thousand undocumented migrants crossed the border every day, and that many of those people were being dispersed across the US by night time plane flights funded by the Biden Administration. With all these folks coming into the US, where will they live? Who will feed, clothe and shelter them? How will they contribute to this country? Whose jobs will they take? Are there terrorist threats among the group?

While all this chaos happened…while the entire world was reeling from the advent of COVID-19…while the federal government was trying to keep its citizens safe from COVID-19, were all these migrants being tested for disease? Who tested these people for COVID-19? AIDS? Encephalitis, etc? Did we just assume that all these people were being vetted for safe entry into our beloved country? From my perspective at DHS HQ, it appeared that few of the new refugees coming from the Southwest Border were being screened for disease as they entered our country.

I will say that there was an attempt to provide some screening for the Afghans coming in. But the government's emphasis was less on health screening and more on "just get them here and we will deal with COVID-19 later". As for the Haitians and the regular migrants coming across the Southwest Border, I saw very few attempts to test them for COVID-19 or any other disease. They could have been bringing in any variety of diseases from COVID-19 to Monkey Pox to Zika, and anything in between.

While all this mayhem is going on in support of filling this country with millions of new refugees, mostly unskilled people who will burden the US economy...there stands tax paying Black Americans in the inner-city. From Atlanta to Los Angeles, inner-city America is dying a slow death from crime, homelessness, crumbling infrastructure, lack of suitable employment, sub-standard education, sub-standard housing, substandard healthcare... the list goes on and on and gets worse every year. If we can spend $100M per day on refugees who have not paid a dime in taxes to this country, why won't this country take care of its own suffering citizens? How come we can send $40 Billion to support war in the Ukraine before we take care of our own American citizens? Shouldn't America value and care for its own tax payers before it offers our precious resources to people who are not citizens of our great country?

Lastly, the most important question is how come Black Americans continue to support a political party that condones and encourages the redistribution and refocusing of America's resources toward non-citizens, while native born Americans continue to struggle?

Why are the elites bringing in so many refugees? Well, I have a couple of theories on that, based on many years working in the Interagency and also, just plain common sense.

These good folks coming across the border mean money to those in power. You see, it's a numbers game. Let's examine the state of Maryland and let's take Baltimore as our example. Congressional seats are allocated based on population, not necessarily citizenship. So, the more people that Baltimore has equates to the more seats Marylanders are allocated in Congress. Those Congressional seats equate to money and resources. If all things were equal, allocating more money to Baltimore would be just dandy. But, to me, it seems that money and resources have been allocated to Baltimore in abundance with diminishing effectiveness, as evidenced by all the crime, corruption and misery reported daily in the local media. Most of the money never reaches the intended recipients.

My next theory involves "Whose jobs are the migrants taking"? The answer is the elites want them here — to replace YOU. A 2019 article in the liberal Washington Post explains that "the only logical conclusion can be the operators want to hire people whose illegal status meant they wouldn't push for higher wages or make trouble". In essence, illegal migrants WORK CHEAP and DON'T COMPLAIN. They do the jobs that Americans don't want to do. Their willingness to do "ugly jobs' keeps prices down. However, in the long run, whose jobs are they taking? Here is another excerpt from the 2019 Washington Post article explaining the situation:

> *"We can also do a lot more to ensure native-born citizens get the first crack at these jobs. One of the raided plants opened in Leake County {Mississippi} in 2017, but apparently there was no concerted effort to ensure these new jobs went to local residents. That's a government failure, as each county has a host of entities tasked with finding jobs for the unemployed, the disabled, mothers on welfare or prisoners reentering the community. These people are our fellow citizens — the ones most in need of the low-skilled, entry-level jobs that undocumented immigrants most often gravitate to. We should be more aggressive about seeking opportunities for these people and pressure local employers to look to these entities first when filling new openings".*[54]

Again, the author stated, "wouldn't it make sense to ensure native-born citizens get the first crack at these jobs?" Well, let's think a little. These jobs are at the lower end of the skills and economic level. Most are dangerous and monotonous, but there is need for them and there is honor in work. Most migrants work hard and don't complain. The companies and the elites who run them want to maximize profit, so they support as much illegal immigration as they can get away with.

The question is, what happened to the people who once did these "dirty jobs" before the migrants came? Most of those folks are Black. So let me get this straight…Black people are voting for the party that takes their jobs away?

That scenario is fine for minorities who can learn a skill and prosper. But what about the large majority of Blacks who don't have marketable skills? Their low skill jobs are underbid by silent, undocumented workers. And most Blacks don't qualify for the higher skilled jobs that the government says are available. Most of those jobs require at least a solid high school education…the same high school education that eludes so many participants in the Baltimore School system. It's a "Catch 22" situation where inner-city Blacks are caught in the middle of a fast-moving river with no paddle. But those same inner-city Blacks continue to support the same system that is virtually drowning them.

Yes, Black Votes Matter

Perhaps, with some change in thinking, Blacks could have a better outcome. Preeminent Stanford Senior Fellow, Dr. Thomas Sowell says that **"Black Votes Matter"**. [55] He believes that "If Republicans could get 20 percent of black votes, the Democrats would be ruined". From what I can see, that figure would apply in Maryland, as well. If Blacks continue to give their votes away to the Democrat party with zero accounting for what the Democrats do with those Black Votes, Black people, especially those in the inner city, should expect the same results. I say, let's make the Democrat Party earn our votes. Let's hold them accountable for their promises and their actions. What have they done for us concerning crime? What have they done for us concerning schools? What have they done for us concerning education? What have they done for us lately? Dr. Sowell thinks that they haven't done much. I agree with Dr. Sowell, who I have been a big fan of since I was a child back in the 70s.

With all that said, do **Black Values Matter? Do Black Votes Matter?** You tell me?

Chapter 4
HOW DID WE GET TO THIS POINT?

Our Grandparents, Their Parents And Your Parents Were Conservatives

I was roughly seven years old during the 1972 Presidential election. I remember a lot of talk in my household among my Grandmother, Grandfather, Mom and Dad. They were conservatives. They were religious, church-going people. They supported Nixon. They saw "Richard Nixon" as their best shot for success. I don't remember exactly what was said, but I remember the term "moral majority", said a few times. I remember them saying something about him trying to get the country out of the war in Vietnam. I didn't understand the words at the time, but I remember my grandmother and most of our church people being supporters of Nixon's campaign. Even James Brown was a Republican. In my house, the Democrats were the party of the hippies. There was respectful talk about Huey Newton and the Black Panthers. Martin and Malcom were revered. But there was also support for Nixon and the traditionalists. What I did not hear was any love for George McGovern, Nixon's opponent. He was considered to be some sort of Northern sissy.

In my home, long serving North Carolina Senator "Jesse Helms" name was synonymous with the Ku Klux Klan. He was absolutely the worst man alive. However, just remember, **he was a Democrat until 1970.** How could such a vile, inhumane person be a DEMOCRAT? How could my family support Nixon, the Republican? How could all of our church members, who I respected and who were friends and relatives of my family, support the "Mean Old Republican"? My normally docile father would get totally spun up at the mere mention of the name "Jesse Helms". My Dad would get really, really heated... literally red in the face.

> ***Originally a Democrat,*** *Helms left the party in 1970. His political transformation was in large part due to his opposition to the Civil Rights Act (1964) that was passed under Pres. Lyndon B. Johnson. In 1972, Helms was elected to the U.S. Senate as a Republican. As senator, he maintained a staunchly conservative stance on social issues, leading a crusade against abortion and homosexuality, supporting prayer in public schools, and opposing the busing of students for racial integration. A polarizing political figure, Helms was reelected four times—in 1978, 1984, 1990, and 1996—but never garnered more than 55 percent of the vote. His campaigns were often criticized for their adversarial tone, as when in 1990, while running against Harvey Gantt, an African American candidate, Helms employed what many considered a blatantly racist television ad that attacked affirmative action.*[56]

Let's review the Reconstruction south of the 1870s. Did you know that the first twenty-three Black Congressmen in this country were "Republicans"?

CHAPTER 4

Yes, it's true. The Republican Party, the Party of Lincoln, was the party that secured liberty for my ancestors. It was the Republican Party that fought to abolish slavery and to preserve the union. It was the Republican Party, not the Democrats, who established the Underground Railroad, supported Fredrick Douglass, Harriet Tubman and the abolitionists of the 1800s…all while the Democrats were establishing and supporting the Ku Klux Klan, the White Citizen's Council and the slave catchers.

- How Did We Go From Being Freed By The Republican Party To Supporting Former Slave Masters, The Democrats?
- How Did Black Americans Become Such Staunch Supporters Of The Very People Who Enslaved And Killed Our Ancestors?

- How Did US History Get So Twisted?

I can give you a short history of the subject. You see, all those stories about the Jim Crow south, Bull Conner, Southern Sovereignty, and all that other "bullshit" started with the Democrat Party after the South was defeated in the Civil War. Some of it continues even today.

Reconstruction and the South.

During Reconstruction, many Blacks took the opportunity to become leaders and even politicians in their communities. Expectedly, there was a lot of poverty and ignorance among the newly emancipated slaves. But just like in any large group, "the cream rose to the top". There were the beginnings of success among the former slaves. Most folks organized around their churches and religious leaders to produce those first twenty-three Black American Congressmen that I mentioned earlier.

Of course, the plantation owners, robber barons and tycoons were not going to stand for recently freed, former slaves to be successful. First, the defender of the Union, President Abraham Lincoln, was martyred. Without Lincoln's vision and leadership, much of the freedoms that had been promised as part of the Civil War were now worthless. The promised "40 Acres And A Mule" was not going to happen. Next begins the Post Civil War, Reconstruction of the South. Now comes the Southern Democrats, the smiling purveyors of the hatred that still serves as the root of so much misery for Black Americans today.

Dixiecrats And The Southern Strategy Believe it or not, Black Americans once overwhelmingly supported the Republican Party.

CHAPTER 4

Yes, it's true. Gradually, they moved to support the Democrat Party between the years of Reconstruction and the early 1960s. As Black Americans moved to the North and West, they found the Democrat Party more aligned with their causes and desires.

> *"In 2016, David Neiwert wrote an article for the Southern Poverty Law Center saying that, "When the members of the Klan were Democrats, as in the 1920s, as well as in the 1940s when they called themselves "Dixiecrats", they were conservative".* [57]

The Democrat Party has a long history of supporting racism and classism, especially in the South. The Democrat Party was the party that supported the secessionists during the civil war. The Republican Party was the party of Abraham Lincoln and Fredrick Douglass. They led the North in the Civil War. Somehow, that story has been switched and Black Americans have bought in to that false narrative.

During Reconstruction, Democrats used hired thugs and political activists to interfere with the hard-won rights of free Black American voters, to include implementing poll taxes and other impediments designed to stifle the Black vote.

Eventually the civil rights struggle showed the philosophical differences between northern and southern Democrats. By 1948, Southern states began to transition from solid Democrat voters to reliable Republican voters. This is when the terms "Dixiecrats" and the "Southern Strategy" came in to common use.

Senator Strom Thurmond was the Dixiecrats' presidential candidate. Note that he became a Republican in 1964. The Dixiecrats represented the weakening of the "Solid South". This action also represented a time of disenfranchisement of Southern Blacks, who were now forced to switch to the Democrat Party or vote against their own interests.

In 1944 and 1948, the Republican Party supported civil rights legislation that the Dixiecrats vigorously opposed in both Congress and in state legislatures across the South. Once again, here is another case where the Democrats actively opposed the cause of civil rights…while the Republicans actively supported the cause of civil rights. Again, how did this get so twisted?

Why Did President Harry Truman Desegregate The Military?

Moving forward to 1948, Dixiecrats (Democrats) opposed President Truman's civil rights legislation. The Dixiecrats intention was to reestablish southern conservative's former leadership and dominance within the national Democrat Party and, perhaps even upset President Harry Truman's reelection bid. Luckily, President Truman was re-elected.

After the 1948 election, the Dixiecrats mostly remained in the Democrat Party. They failed in their bid to replace President Truman but managed to cause a schism in the Democrat Party that paved the way for the dominance of the Republican Party in the southern United States that holds to this very day.

Furthermore, millions of Black Americans served in World War II, both in the military and as civilian workers. They learned their value to the country through their war effort. The earned pay equal to that of their majority counterparts and they were not about to return home from the war and accept second class citizenship in a country they had just fought for. They would no longer stand for Poll Taxes, Jim Crow laws and the Status Quo.

In summary, the true narrative is that President Truman signed Executive Order 8802,[58] desegregating the U.S. military as a result of a complicated turn of events that allowed him to get just enough votes to defeat the segregationist, conservative Dixiecrats led by the evil race-baiter, Strom Thurmond. Also of note is that President Roosevelt, who Black Democrats still revere, never tried to desegregate the military during his four terms as President.

The military was desegregated as a necessity for the Democrats to remain in power, not as a result of any great need for justice. Truman, a Democrat, was a pragmatic President who used the votes of Black Americans to stay in office.[59]

Let's review: deceased Klansman and former West Virginia Senator Robert Byrd; deceased race-baiting Senator Strom Thurmond; the Crooked Clintons; and Old Joe Biden, master of the disastrous 1994 Crime Bill, and the man who said, "if you have a problem figuring out whether you're for me or Trump, then you ain't Black"[60]; all these sketchy politicians are Democrats. Black Americans supported Democrat politicians like these for decades, and got little from them. Please tell me again what Black Americans owe the Democrats? Please tell me again if **Black Values Matter?**

Chapter 5
HOW WE FIX BALTIMORE
(And Inner-City America)

Let's Put The Charm Back In Charm City

Hollis Albert and Ken Rochon are friends of mine. They, and a few others of our crew, are committed to making positive changes in Baltimore. Hollis managed my congressional campaign. Through my campaign efforts, I met Ken, who happens to make a living as a book publisher. These men have long term ties to Baltimore. They see the carnage, and they, like me, are willing to take action to help change things. But the question is, how do we do it?

Hollis really knows local business and government, having run bars, restaurants and even an oil company. He once served as the City's Fire Commissioner. He is very involved in Baltimore's Republican political scene and he knows a whole gang of good people on both sides of the political aisle, who want to see positive changes in Baltimore and in the region.

Ken Rochon is an entrepreneur. He publishes books. He hosts a podcast. He is officially registered with the National Press Club as a photographer. As a hobby, he even dabbles in stand-up comedy. He is a true "Renaissance Man". He and I met on the campaign trail about fifty miles west of Baltimore. As we chatted, we discovered a mutual interest in "Saving Baltimore" and that we shared a sense of egalitarian values. We also discovered that we live about a mile from each other. The next thing you know, Ken, Hollis and I were plotting on what we call, "Commitment, Charm City, Incorporated". Our goal with Commitment, Charm City, Incorporated (CCCI) is to change the attitude of Baltimore's residents towards the positive. How will we do that? We, like any good initiative, must do it one person at a time.

We know what doesn't work. An unbroken line of Liberal progressive leadership has been in the Mayor's office since 1967. The high taxes and dependence on the government that come with progressive liberal leadership has led to decades of misery for the citizens. It's led to failing schools. It's led to high crime and a whole lot of other negatives that have people leaving the city in droves.

Hard core Republican leadership would probably fair no better. That is why the poorest people of the city scoff at Republican leaders who even attempt to offer a different way to govern. Most of the people of the city see Republicans as "the enemy" no matter what we say. The idea of "pulling yourself up by your bootstraps" is a foreign concept to people who have "no boots".

In truth, the people of Baltimore were handed a big, greasy "shit sandwich" but they were told it would be a "crab cake" by the people who they elected. Those in charge only want to maintain "the status quo", no matter what they say. It's a sad treatise on today's politics, but as long as poor people remain poor, they are literally powerless.

CHAPTER 5

How do we change this situation? Could we bring in more money and government programs? Well, that tactic has failed before. The money doesn't get to the people. It ends up in the hands of middle men, race hustlers, bureaucrats and various poverty-pimps who stand between the people and their needs. If you don't believe me, then why do Baltimore City Schools have the highest per pupil spending in the state (roughly $22K per year), but the worst educational outcomes in the state. All the while, the administrators in the city school system drive the most expensive cars in the parking lot and generally make twice the salaries of the teachers. Or, what happened to the $1.5B President Obama gave Baltimore [61] before he left office. $1.5B should have made a positive impact in the city. Where is the "Hope and Change" in Baltimore City Schools?

The mission statement our new "Commitment, Charm City, Incorporated is: To Research, Investigate And Develop Strategies And Coalitions To Improve The Governance, Management And Lives Of Baltimore City Residents And Visitors.

There are some eighty-one departments governing Baltimore City that have not provided for an efficient, modern, operational city. From schools, safety, water, promotion of tourism, recreation and parks, including almost every other department, the management provided by the bureaucrats, council members and Mayor's office is not just lacking, but a failure. Instead of just starting another 501(c)(3) organization and doing nothing, you can expect that we will accomplish positive actions. We secured a brand-new board of bi-partisan business owners and citizens who are ready to lead positive change in Baltimore. We recently received our charter, and you will be hearing about us. We are committed to bridging the political gaps between conservatives and liberals, and leading positive change in Baltimore. Our website can be found at www.commitmentcharmcity.org. Join us.

Let's Treat Our Fellow Humans As We Want To Be Treated

In the fall of 2021, I was appointed to Maryland's State Judicial Nominating Commission, where I help to select judges in the 9th district. I had some free time on my hands and wanted to help my fellow citizens. My politically involved friends recommended that I submit my name to the governor's office, as a volunteer for one of the "boards" that go unfilled every year.

I polished up my resume and submitted it, thinking that, considering my work history, I would be considered for a board position on cyber security, information technology or veterans affairs. A few months after my submission, the governor's office offered me a position on the Trial Courts Nomination Commission for District 9, Howard County. This group recommends judicial appointments to the Governor. The group consists of twelve people with a legal background, along with three non-lawyers sprinkled in to offer the perspective of a layman…a private citizen…an interested party who is not involved in the legal business.

I met with this group for the first time in the fall of 2021. I was still working for DoD at the time, so I had to take leave to attend. I went to Howard County's sprawling, brand new county courthouse for the meeting. I was impressed. I have lived in Howard County over fourteen years and had never needed to go to the County Courthouse. I guess that is a good thing.

CHAPTER 5

The board members arrived roughly fifteen minutes early, as is customary. As I walked in, they all seemed to know each other from working together in the past. I didn't say much, just observing, as is typical for me around strangers. Everyone was polite and professional as we reviewed the resumes and speeches of the candidates.

We reviewed eight or ten candidates. Some appeared more qualified than others, as is the norm. What struck me is the case of one candidate who was more than qualified, in my opinion. He was a West Point Graduate; an Army Ranger who re-trained into the Army Legal Corps. This man had been an Army Lawyer for a decade and for some reason decided to leave the Army prior to retirement in order to pursue a successful civilian legal career. The man's resume and background were impeccable…just the kind of resume that would make an outstanding, long serving judge.

As he came up for the interview, "Bob" was reserved and knowledgeable, as he answered questions. After his testimony, he left the room. Then the group discussed his background, resume and testimony.

As we deliberated, it was clear to me that Bob was the most qualified candidate with the best resume and responses we saw that day. However, the consensus opinion of the crowd was that he was "arrogant". To me, I saw that as "he is a White Man and therefore, not qualified".

I took offense to that observation. I left my mode of quiet observance and went into defense mode. I made a little speech on behalf of a man who I didn't know. From my perspective, why was the most qualified applicant that we had being disqualified because he just happened to have skin that didn't look like mine or he didn't have the correct gender? To me, that is the epitome of discrimination. What I saw was a man who had survived the crucible of West Point, the elimination chamber of Army Ranger School and who had a decade of judicial experience, both in and outside of DoD. When the group asked my opinion of his supposed arrogance, I explained as follows;

> *"I don't know this man, but I share a commonality with him, serving as a military officer during war time. This man served in the Army Infantry as a Ranger. Like me, he was expected to make life and death decisions involving his subordinates. What you are perceiving as arrogance is actually the kind of confidence and surety that will help him adhere to the law when pressured. As a military officer charged with keeping his troops alive and also accomplishing his assigned mission, he cannot afford to show emotion under pressure. This county would be well served to have "Bob" as a judge".*

As a result of my impromptu speech, "Bob's" resume was among three packages forwarded to the governor as a judicial nominee. "Bob" eventually was not selected by the governor, but on that day, my words made the difference that moved his package forward.

It concerned me that these pleasant, educated, accomplished people seemed biased against a fellow human being. They saw him as "a typical privileged White guy". I saw him as a human being with a superior resume and a superior presentation, who just happened to be the best qualified person that was presented to our board. I understand the need to balance racial scales. But at some point, placing minorities in positions of power just because they are minorities reaches the law of diminishing returns.

Didn't MLK challenge us to "Judge people by the content of their character, and not by the color of their skin"? Didn't MLK also say that, "Injustice anywhere is a threat to justice everywhere"? In our attempt to balance racial scales, is it fair to judge people in ways that our ancestors were once judged? I believe that people should be judged on their merits and not on their skin color or their sexuality. A flawed system can't be fixed by even more biases. Otherwise, we risk perpetuating the same discrimination that has divided this country since its founding. That makes us no better than the old southern racists that I grew up with.

Homeless Baltimore

Speaking of the Golden Rule, we have far too many homeless people in Baltimore and America's inner-cities. They are camping on the medians of busy streets. They are panhandling. They are intimidating tourists and visitors. Can we help them find permanent housing?

I noticed several huge, new looking apartment buildings in the heart of the city. Those buildings appear to be recently renovated, but the windows were boarded up. I asked my friend why those buildings were unoccupied, since he lives in the city and should know. My friend said that those buildings were privately owned and the city had little influence over them.

I saw this same thing happen in DC where I once worked. It's called "gentrification». Corporations and individuals, who can afford to, purchase distressed properties and wait for the residents to move away from the crime and lack of supporting infrastructure. When the residents leave, the owners turn the property in to high rent condos. The residents who can't afford to live in those expensive new buildings are forced out. "Gentrification" is quietly changing the character of America's cities.

I was in West Baltimore recently. As my buddy and I drove through the streets, I noticed dozens of huge, dilapidated townhouses. We agreed that most of the dilapidated housing was "Structurally Sound", only needing renovation to meet city codes and be viable family structures again. In fact, several of those buildings had been refurbished and were serving as active homes for families. That is great. However, far too many had not been refurbished. On the same trip, I spoke to a couple of young contractors who were trying to "flip" some of those properties. They were putting in "sweat equity" to improve the neighborhood, while trying to make a profit. I applaud their efforts. But, the general consensus among them was that city code made it nearly impossible to make a profit on their work. To these entrepreneurs, city government was making it harder for them to improve properties that they were actually living in. Baltimore's Byzantine construction rules make it difficult for residents to improve their own properties.

With the billions that Baltimore gets from the Federal and State government, wouldn't it make sense for the city to buy those vacant buildings, using "Imminent Domain" laws to ensure residents have adequate housing? Otherwise, soon Baltimore will no longer be "Baltimore" as the city's people are forced to leave. Who profits from poor people leaving the inner-city? Could it be that some of our elites don't really want to improve problems with Crime, Education, Affordable Housing, Homelessness, etc.? Could it be that they prefer to turn a profit instead?

I believe that the city should prioritize the ownership of single-family homes, as opposed to building monstrous apartment buildings.

Our priority should be for "owner-occupants" as opposed to "land lords" who live outside the city and the state. It's proven that owners care about neighborhoods more than renters. Let's encourage "home ownership" in Baltimore. Let's ensure that we incentivize real estate developers and bankers who are from our counties and from our state, before we bring in real estate developers who are not from our state. We should reward businesses who have "Skin In The Game" so to speak. We should reward businesses who have the best interests of Baltimore's residents in mind.

Let's Reform Our Police

Another goal that can improve Charm City is reforming the Police. Neither the populace, nor the police force in Baltimore are happy. At last check, the city police force is down 800+ officers. Peace Officers don't want to work under the premise of "Defund the Police". The way things are, most people don't want to become Peace Officers. It's a dangerous, thankless, low paying job. I have been in war zones that are safer than the streets of West Baltimore. And no, the police are not perfect. Many of them have a well-earned bad reputation. But they are what stands between order and chaos in the city. Instead of constant criticism of the police force, why not support them so they can do a better job for our citizens. Here are a few of my ideas:

- Let's rebrand them as "Peace Officers" since they are employed to keep the Peace. Let's raise the number of Peace Officers, not reduce the number. If there is money in our budgets to support endless foreign wars, there is money in our budget to support the war on our inner-city streets.
- Let's support Peace Officers legislatively. Taking away their "qualified immunity" was a slap in the face and has

encouraged many city Peace Officers to resign their positions. As a result, police are afraid to do their jobs and the citizens are less safe.
- Let's do a better job of screening and recruiting Peace Officers. My impression is that many of the people seeking law enforcement jobs have a "Bully Complex" (i.e., seeking to rule over others). People like that should not serve as Peace Officers. Psychological tests that can weed those people out of the hiring pool are available.
- Fully funding the universal use of body cameras would go a long way toward ensuring that Peace Officers execute their jobs effectively and efficiently.
- Emphasizing the use of de-escalation procedures, instead of the old psychological control tactics might help Peace Officers better relate to the communities they serve.
- States Attorney Maryland Mosby lost her latest election. Her defeat and departure will go a long way towards reestablishing trust and good will between Baltimore's citizens and its Peace Officers. Her policies served to increase lawlessness in the city. Her departure is a step in the right direction.

Should We Bring In The National Guard?

An Aug 2022 article in Hot Air Magazine stated that "NAACP asks for National Guard to be deployed in Baltimore". "The NAACP has petitioned the Governor to declare a public state of emergency in Baltimore and deploy the National Guard to get the violence under control".[62] Have things gotten so bad in Charm City that we need to deploy "The Military" in order to police our streets? Is the progressive liberal establishment that has led

Baltimore for decades admitting defeat? As of the writing of the article, roughly 230 murders have occurred this year. That number is expected to be well over 300 by the end of 2022.

Mayor Brandon Scott promised to execute a five-year plan to reduce murder and crime, but so far all he has done is blame entities other than himself.

What is happening here? Blacks are in charge of most of the powerful political offices in Baltimore, but things have not improved for our inner-city. They have asked for and received the votes of the people of Baltimore, yet they fail to deliver on their campaign promises.

The 2022 governor's race just concluded. Let's review the current state of the governorship on crime reduction in Baltimore;

- Governor Hogan's policies have done little to stem the tide of crime in Baltimore during his two terms as Maryland's governor.
- Governor-Elect Wes Moore has shown no plan to stem the tide of crime and violence in the city. I don't see anything specific in his platform that indicates that he will do anything different from his Uni-Party mates. From what I see of his platform and his speeches, and the fact that he has never held elected office, we can expect the same ignorance from him that we have gotten from the rest of the progressive wing of the Democrat party.

Crime has been a big factor in Charm City for decades. Has the time come for the National Guard to patrol Baltimore's streets? Perhaps the NAACP is correct in their recommendation? Perhaps they are not. But, if so, how come the NAACP is so wedded to the Democrat Party. Why not hold the Democrat Party and its political leaders accountable, since they have been in charge of Baltimore for over five decades?

By the way, I am not in favor of deploying the National Guard to patrol Baltimore's streets. Deploying the National Guard would take the Charm out of Charm City. It would indicate "the failure" of our civil government. As a military officer, I am all too familiar with the downside of implementing "Martial Law". Except in the case of a natural disaster or other unforeseen contingency, we Veterans of Foreign Wars will never support suspending American citizen's rights on our own soil. Successful "Best of Breed" crime reduction models exist in this country. We should find one that fits Baltimore and implement it.

My friend Dee lives in the heart of Baltimore. She is a community advocate, deeply involved and engaged in the happenings of the city. Here is her account of some of the crime in her neighborhood in late August 2022;

- *Last week a perp with a warrant on him entered the front of Southern District HQ. When they searched him, they found a loaded gun with three loaded clips. He could've slaughtered all of the cops in the HQ.*
- *There should be metal detectors at entrances to police buildings. The cops at the front desk are unarmed, assigned to light duty for various reasons. They are sitting ducks.*
- *Cops working overtime are not getting paid. They're not volunteering or signing up for overtime anymore. They are being forced to work 16-20 hour days.*

- *Officers are driving broken down cruisers that are over 10 years old.*
- *A drug dealer was shot 20 times. A 17 yr old neighbor caught a stray bullet in the head from the gunfire.*
- *The other night, 200 people were fighting in the streets. Ten cops were sent to manage the crowd.*
- *My cop friend was in a fist fight with a perp @ Fells Point. He hurt his shoulder and his elbow. He got written up by the lieutenant because he didn't properly introduce himself!*
- *Consent decree has got to go. Hundreds more will die before January.*

Dee, Baltimore Resident. (24 Aug 2022.)

What Have the Democrat's Done for Baltimore Lately?

Successive Democrat-run administrations have left Baltimore with entrenched, unlivable crime, corruption and urban blight. Why do we continue to support this failed party without at least considering another approach.

The Federal government has a big role to play. For example, the Federal government once tried to restrict people from the use of alcohol. I assume that its intentions were good however, the government's efforts resulted in the historic violence of Al Capone and the gangsters of 1930's America. I believe much of today's inner-city crime stems from the Federal government's failed War On Drugs. The War on Drugs started roughly fifty years ago during the Nixon administration, creating another useless, burgeoning federal bureaucracy that has encouraged a black market for drugs and brought unprecedented violence and crime to

America's inner-city neighborhoods. This wasted effort should be stopped and the billions of excess dollars should be repurposed to fund more useful grassroots efforts.

One historical fact I must mention is the in-pouring of drugs into inner city communities to fund the Iran-Contra operation. Our own government "condoned, if not actively supported...the Nicaraguan contras in their drug dealing", as evidenced by a series of stories by San Jose Mercury News reporter Gary Webb, back in 1996.[63] Our governments activities eventually led to more brutal policing and the three strikes laws that (then Vice President) Bush, Clinton and Biden proposed. Many Black men were imprisoned for crack, while Majority Wall Street types openly lived on cocaine (Hunter Biden still does). Citizens need balanced and fair policing, instead of defunding police. Both extremes are polarizing and do not contribute to positive change.

With that said, Baltimore has been run by Democrats since 1967. With near universal political power in the hands of Democrats and billions of federal dollars spent on Baltimore and inner-cities, how have the lives of inner-city residents improved, as compared to other parts of the country?

Let's Fix Our Schools

You go to a restaurant and order a steak. You tell the wait staff exactly what you want, and you are ready to pay for it. You expect a good experience. But you don't get what you expected. The steak comes to you cold and undercooked. It looks unappetizing. What's more is, the wait staff has an attitude of "don't you dare question this food or my service". What do you do? Do you complain? Do you come back to that same restaurant tomorrow and go through the same experience? If you choose the latter, perhaps the fault is not with the restaurant, but with you.

We are experiencing a similar situation with Baltimore's school system. Citizens are paying top dollar for unsatisfactory results. Citizens are getting a poor meal, but we are continuing to patronize the same restaurant. There is little competition among Baltimore's public schools. The fault lies with us, the customer, for not holding the schools accountable.

I don't know of anyone who is happy with the Baltimore City's School Systems, yet we continue to follow the same failed path that is producing high school graduates who cannot contribute to society. It's hard to talk about but it's true. Baltimore's schools have earned a well-deserved poor reputation. Our efforts to educate Baltimore's children have not produced positive results. How do we achieve the positive results that Maryland's citizens expect and deserve? How can we change Baltimore City School's poor reputation?

A good statement of the problem comes from Jovani and Shawnda Patterson, a Baltimore couple who filed a federal lawsuit on behalf of Baltimore's citizens, alleging that city residents received "no benefit" from a school system that "completely fails to perform its most important function" of educating Baltimore's children.[64] The lawsuit lists a variety of complaints including; "poor student performance"; a "pattern" of enrollment and grading scandals"; "making false entries in public records; racketeering; mail fraud, theft; embezzlement"; "advancing students without equipping them with the knowledge needed to succeed at the next grade level".

The Maryland Office of the Inspector General, after a three-year investigation, found that Baltimore City Public Schools were party to more than twelve thousand failing grades being changed to passing grades over a period of five years. Baltimore TV Station WMAR's article from June 2022, stated that "at nearly 130 Baltimore City Schools between grades six through twelve, 12,552 grades were changed from failing to passing." [65] How can we expect the next generation of children to lead our nation when our school systems socially promote them…when we lie to the kids and make them think that they are ready to contribute to society? Underperforming public schools in Baltimore and most of urban America are weakening our country and our children's future.

The Teacher's Union (Teacher's Mafia) and the US Department of education redistribute billions of tax payer dollars into failing public schools across our nation. In those cases where the schools are not properly serving our kids, we should implement **School Choice**.[66] The roughly $22K per child spent on kids' education in Baltimore should be given to parents for them to decide what school their kids should attend. There are many great charter schools and private schools that can produce a better outcome for Baltimore's children than what is offered now. With more competition and accountability, perhaps we can improve the performance of Baltimore City's Schools.

A couple of months ago, I attended a demonstration at the Baltimore City Schools Head Quarters (HQ). There was television coverage and a speech from the Deputy Superintendent of the school system. I was there to observe, so I kept my mouth shut. One gentleman "expressed his opinion". He was angry, to say the least. As the Deputy Superintendent started his speech, the man interrupted. He was a Black man, appearing to be in his late 30's. He was very, very upset…almost violent.

He told the story of how he had attended city schools and through grading, was given the impression that he would be able to make a good living for himself after graduation. After he took the SAT, with the intention of attending college, he discovered that his high school had not come close to preparing him to attend any college. He took the military's Armed Services Vocational Aptitude Battery (ASVAB) and found out that he was woefully unqualified for virtually any job in the military. He was "functionally illiterate" after twelve years of attending city schools. He attributes his misfortune to the Baltimore City School System. His story is typical.

I felt badly for the man but I didn't feel badly for the deputy school superintendent. The deputy failed to answer any of the man's questions as the television cameras rolled. Eventually, the superintendent literally ran from the gaze of the camera and went to hide within the HQ building. To my knowledge, he still hidden in there today.

So again, how do we fix Baltimore City's schools? How do we get people to understand that the government is not interested in solving their problems…that the government will only give you enough resources to stay poor. How do we promote self-sufficiency? Consequently, how do we get politicians to understand that the people of Baltimore are proud Americans who deserve to live with dignity, safety and respect? How do we get people to take active control of their lives?

Let's Take Charge Of Our Children's Educations

Many school boards are infiltrated by Leftists, and even Marxists, who think that children belong to the state instead of their parents. Our kids are being indoctrinated into believing that our great western culture is somehow bad. Marxists are literally trying to replace our American Culture. If they are allowed to hold sway, your lifestyle will change in a negative and irretrievable fashion. Moreover, your children are being indoctrinated against you, the parents.

We must legally oppose Leftists at every opportunity. Critical Race Theory, Gender Neutral Philosophy and Leftism are divisive and will not serve our country well in the future. I recommend you get involved in your children's educations. Schools should teach reading, writing and math, not racial division. Your children are being molded. Ensure they are molded into what you want them to be.

Can The Republicans Be More Inclusive?

Recently, I attended the Maryland Grand Old Party's (MDGOP) Annual Gala and Fundraiser. I paid $200 to attend, which I thought was quite an exorbitant fee for such an event. My friend and campaign manager, Hollis, and I went together, grudgingly forking over the $200 per plate price tag. It was held at a swanky hotel, and there were a many well-heeled guests there. But I was not impressed.

Former Trump administration insider Kelly Anne Conway, gave an inspiring keynote speech. I even picked up one of her books. She was very impressive, but still, I was not impressed. At an event that was sponsored by a Grand Old Party that claims to want to look more like today's America, I witnessed an event attended by very

CHAPTER 5

few people who looked like me out of the roughly 500 people in the room.

I am not saying that there should be a 13% quota, matching the Black population of the US, but I expected to see more than the roughly ten people of color that I counted. And, half of those ten were on the wait staff. What's worse is that the tables were color coded by ticket cost. The tickets started at $200 and moved higher from there. To me, this looked like the same old segregation and separation that keeps people thinking of the Grand Old Party as "The Party Of The Rich".

I was told that several wealthy, prominent Democrats were in attendance, sitting right up front. Our two-hundred-dollar tickets got Hollis and me cheap seats at the far edge of the room. I likened our seat placement to the way the MDGOP treats the members of its party. They want the votes of the people, but when decisions are made, the people become window dressing. Hollis joked about feeling like he was "Sitting At The Back Of The Bus". Middle Class families saving to pay for their kid's college, paying for daycare, running small businesses, etc. (the GOP's target voters) should not have to pay that kind of money to support their party. If we expect them to support us, we must make things more affordable for them.

How could the Maryland GOP have made this event more inclusive? If they want to inspire and secure voters, why not have more than one gala per year? Some GOP members like me will pay $200 per ticket, but most won't pay more than that. In order to make the event more inclusive, why not host more events with more affordable tickets. That way, more of the Middle-Class voters that the GOP counts as its constituents might consider attending.

Next, why not hold events at multiple locations. Annapolis, College Park and Baltimore are great locations, but the folks out in Frederick Maryland and those folks up in Hampstead and Manchester need some love, too. The folks from across the Chesapeake Bay Bridge might like some attention, as well. I would bet that several of the GOP Central Committees would have been willing to partner to host annual galas in their areas, had they been asked. Instead, the MDGOP holds one annual gala for the "elite of the elites". Also, who is sure that any of the funds raised reached any of the candidates? Not good. Not good at all. We need more transparency in the MDGOP.

Again, what I saw was a homogeneous group of elites who didn't reach out to potential voters. After attending this MDGOP gala, I predicted that the GOP would pay dearly for their slight at Maryland's polls. And, I was right. On Election Day, 2022, "The Red Wave" didn't happen. Maybe the ticket price of supporting Maryland's Republican Party was just too high?

The Democrats host their tiered fundraisers as well. But the Democrat elites hide their contempt for the lower classes much better than the Republican elites do. If the GOP wants to win elections in Maryland or anywhere else, it must supplant the Democrats as "the Party of America's Working People". The Republican Party must be strategic and coordinated in its actions. Otherwise, the GOP will continue to lose winnable elections. At this point, neither the Democrats nor the Republicans appear to be looking out for middle class people. The GOP must change its ways if it wants to win. I see this time as a prime opportunity to change the politics in this whole state.

Before I ran for Congress, Hollis and I reached out to the MDGOP for advice and support. The MDGOP ignored us. At one point, I was the only Republican Congressional Candidate registered to run in District 2. On the last day for candidates to file to run, the MDGOP submitted their own candidate, along with encouraging other candidates to run. All of a sudden, five new candidates showed up out of nowhere, at the last minute.

I spent $35K of my own money and we raised another $20K for our campaign. The result of all this political skullduggery was yet another loss to the now, ten term Democrat incumbent. I am certain that he will continue to bring the same "hope and change" to his district. Perhaps with a little support, guidance and coordination from the MDGOP, my team and I might have won.

There are good people in our party who would make fine, winning candidates, but our party leadership appears to be interested only in maintaining the status quo. That means the Republicans will continue to lose. Many Blacks, Hispanics and Asians are church-going conservatives. Many of them are immigrants. Those communities are looking to partner with conservatives. Many of them are very, very patriotic. They came to America for Freedom. I saw lots of them recently, especially the South Asians and East Asians. The MDGOP doesn't appear to have made much of a pitch for their votes. If the GOP wants to win, it can't ignore any voter. The MDGOP must recruit them.

What am I doing to help this situation since I have so much to say? On 10 Oct 2022, Commitment, Charm City, Inc. hosted an event in Central Baltimore for our gubernatorial candidates, with advertising targeted specifically to Democrats and Independents. We wanted to give inner-city residents a chance to meet them, to ask them questions and get to know them. We invited the Democrat's nominee and his Lt Governor candidate, but they turned us down.

Of the invited candidates, only the GOP's Lt Governor candidate attended. What a missed opportunity.

What's important is that we, the political parties, need to make ourselves available at the grassroots level. The elites who attended the MDGOP fundraiser are wealthy, but they have only one vote apiece. I want the GOP to be the party that cares about regular folks and regular folk's problems; not the party of the elites. It's time for the Republicans to stop looking down on working class people. It's time for the Republican Party to reclaim its roots and take its rightful place as part of the solution.

Let's Keep Smiling

My buddy Ken has a portion of the solution. We must make people SMILE. Has anyone ever mistreated you while they were SMILING? Only a sociopath will smile at you while they are harming you. We need to bring more SMILES to the city. Those smiles…simple as they may be…will serve to change people's attitudes. Those smiles will empower the good people and disarm the bad people. I have seen it during my travels all over this world. I was at a comedy club recently. Everyone was in a good mood, smiling and relaxed. No one meant anyone any drama. Everyone in the club was on their best behavior. All was well. This happens more often than not. Studies show that smiling "disarms" people. Just a simple smile can change the direction of the city. And, a smile costs nothing.

Our intention is to gather up some volunteers and blanket the city with cards that say, "Keep Smiling". I have personally passed "Keep Smiling" cards out to random strangers. In most cases, people take

CHAPTER 5

the card and immediately change their scowl to a smile. If we blanket the city with our "Keep Smiling" cards, maybe we can stop some of the ugliness that happens in the city. Even if we save just one person from a bad day, it will be worth it. As we change the attitude of the city…as we substitute positive vibrations for negative vibrations, maybe we can save some lives. Just think about it. We aren't asking for money. We are asking for SMILES.

SUMMARY
(The Beginning Of Better Days)

Many people will say, "that's all simple...anyone can say what Berney said." Well, the things that I have laid out here are "easier said than done". If these things were so easy to do, little old ladies could walk the streets of West Baltimore at midnight without fear. Until such time as this, we have work to do. We should look within and determine what WE can do as individuals to make things better.

Below is a bulletized summary of my ideas to improve Baltimore, and in turn, move America and its urban communities towards safety, peace and prosperity.

- Follow The "Golden Rule" By Treating Others As You Wish To Be Treated.
- Improve Public Safety By Reforming And Re-Funding Police Departments.
- End The War On Drugs.
- Fix Schools By Offering School Choice.
- Foster Excellence Among Schools By Allowing Funding To Follow Students.
- Get Involved In Local Politics, Be It Democrat, Republican, Independent, etc.

- Keep Smiling. It's Contagious.
- Hold Yourself Accountable For Your Life. Strive To Live Your Best Life.

I can't fix these problems alone. If we want positive results, each of us must take personal responsibility to do what is right for his or her respective family and community. Trust me, I will do my part. My close friends know that my word is my bond. I try to live by the phrase, "Lead, Follow, Or Get Out Of The Way." Maybe I will run for office again. And, if I am elected, I will do exactly as I promised, to the best of my ability.

Before we blame "The Majority" or "The Immigrants", or "The Elites" or someone else for our respective lot in life, I recommend we look in the mirror and take responsibility for our own happiness. Only you know what you have done to "live your best life".

So, after all these words, **Do Black Values Matter?** Only you can answer that question. In this book, I have touched on the concepts of Black Culture, politics, our government's failures, Black History and my plan to fix America's Inner-Cities. This book is an essay on how I see life and my thoughts on how to make life better for all Americans. The most important thing that I wish to leave you with is the concept of "The Golden Rule". We should treat others as we wish to be treated. If we focus on improving our own civility, our own character and own work ethic, then the blessings we seek will come to us. If we can implement these principles, perhaps **Black Values Will Matter.**

ACKNOWLEDGEMENTS

To my War Dawgs...whether we met during my military career or during my DoD civilian career or anywhere in between, thanks for rolling with me. You know who you are. I value you; I treasure our friendship and I look forward to seeing you all again very soon.

To my Campaign Team, Commitment Charm City, Inc. and my Political Buddies; we have known each other less than two years and you have become a new family for me. You are my trusted ideological North Star. Let's do some good together. In no particular order;

> Mr. Hollis Albert, Mr. and Ms. Will and Beth Lawson, Dr. Ray Serrano, Dr. Ken Rochon, Ms. Jolie McShane, Ms. Kira Winne, Dr. Charlene Jenkins, Dr. Frank Nice, Mr. Tommy Carrigan, Special Agent Rick Fiesel (Ret), Colonel Vince Crabb (Ret), Ms. Angela Lane, Lieutenant Colonel Khris Greene (Ret), Dr. Joe Mufareh, Ms. Donna Rzepka, Ms. Blanca Tapahuasco, Ms. Tien Nguyen, Ms. Mercedes Mobius, Ms. Gordana Schifanelli, Esq., Mr. Vincent Chaigne, Ms. Cathey Allison, Petty Officer Jeremey Washington, Mr. Justin Taylor, Delegate (Colonel) Reid Novotny, Delegate Dan Cox Esq., Mr. And Mrs Ed and Heather Berlett, Coach Tony DeCesare, Ms. Annie Sanford, Ms. Amy Leahy, LTC. Tom Kennedy, Esq., Ms. Kate Sullivan, Ms. Blaire Freed, Chief Petty Officer

Mallory Bramlett, Colonel Mark Aldrich, Major Bill Gripp, Lieutenant Colonel Cail Morris (Ret), Master Sergeant Ed Perry (Ret), Mr. Mark Campabello, Dr. Eric Clemons, Lieutenant Colonel Ron Thornton (Ret), Commander Patrick Grady (Ret), Ms. Linda McClooney, Mr and Mrs. Merrill and Deb Thomas, Ms. Angela Lane, Mr. and Ms. Greg and Lisa Malveaux, Dr. Mariela Roca, Lt Col Calvin Bowditch (Ret), Mr. And Ms. Kenny and Zulicka Basemore, Mr. John May, Mr. Chris Anderson, Ms. Blair Freed, Ms. Maria Zickuhr, Rev. And Ms. Derek and Linda Bell, Colonel Dwayne Dickens (Ret), Colonel Karlton Johnson (Ret), Ms. Loraine Bezilla, Brigadier General Bear Ard (Ret), Dr. Colonel Hal Arata (Ret), Chief Master Sergeant John Nelams (Ret) and Senior Master Sergeant Katie Nelams(Ret), Major Greg Martin (Ret), Mr. and Mrs. Eric and Susan Wells, Lieutenant Colonel Tim Valledares (Ret), Command Master Chief Jay Terry (Ret) and Ms. Sandra Terry, the Janvier Family, the Dector Family, Metro Conservative Media, The Tri-District Republican Club, Republican Women's Club of Baltimore County, Central Baltimore County Republican Club, The Republican Club of Baltimore City, The Patriot Club of Baltimore, Carroll County Republican Victory, The Central Baltimore County Republican Club, Cyber Task Force, etc.

This list is not even close to complete. If I didn't list your name, I will make it up to you in the next book

MORE FROM BERNEY

Upon realizing that our great country was digressing in many ways, I decided to "be the change that I wanted to see" by running for Congress. I campaigned as a first-time candidate in the 2nd District of Maryland, losing in the Republican primary.

As a military service member, on several occasions I was honored to deploy to various war zones in defense of my country. I was stationed at the Pentagon during the infamous 9/11 terrorist attack. I am a first-generation college graduate, earning a Master's degree in Public Administration, graduating from the US Air Force War College, and earning multiple graduate certificates in various disciplines. I am an active mentor, particularly of young men, most importantly, I spent my life seeking truth as a follower of Jesus Christ.

Growing up, I was destined to be just another statistic. I was a typical chubby, dark-skinned black kid from the poorest county in the State of North Carolina. I was introverted, preferring cartoons and comic books to the real world. In my early teens, I once overheard my father say to my mother, "that boy ain't gonna make it".

My father was a quiet, industrious man who worked at a local textile mill and farmed his family's land as a side-hustle. His plan for me was to join him on "the line" at Burlington Mills, marry, raise some kids and die on Tobacco Road.

My mother had other plans for me, my brother and sister. She demanded the best from us academically and spiritually, and expected that we would make her proud one day. As a result, all three of her children have grown up, married, built great families and become successful in their own right. Her three children all have traditional families with "until death do you part" marriages. We are proud people, taught to honor our family name and those who came before us.

REFERENCES

8 Important Statistics that Black America Needs To Recognize Now. (2011, February 9). MadameNoire. https://madamenoire.com/107615/8-important-statistics-that-black-america-should-pay-attention-to-now/4/

Access Denied. (2012a, May 28). https://thegrio.com/2012/05/28/harry-truman-and-the-desegregation-of-the-military-a-timeline/

Access Denied. (2012b, May 28). https://thegrio.com/2012/05/28/harry-truman-and-the-desegregation-of-the-military-a-timeline/

africa-during-the-scramble-the-amazon-s-last-stand. (n.d.). https://www.sealionpress.co.uk/post/africa-during-the-scramble-the-amazon-s-last-stand. https://www.sealionpress.co.uk/post/africa-during-the-scramble-the-amazon-s-last-stand

african-slave-castles.html. (n.d.). https://lasentinel.net/african-slave-castles.html. https://lasentinel.net/african-slave-castles.html

Applications Open for Baltimore's Guaranteed Income Pilot Program. (2022, May 2). Mayor Brandon M. Scott. https://mayor.baltimorecity.gov/news/press-releases/2022-05-02-

applications-open-baltimore%E2%80%99s-guaranteed-income-pilot-program

Archie, A. (2022a, September 20). *Joe Biden says the COVID-19 pandemic is over. This is what the data tells us.* NPR.org. https://www.npr.org/2022/09/19/1123767437/joe-biden-covid-19-pandemic-over

Archie, A. (2022b, September 20). *Joe Biden says the COVID-19 pandemic is over. This is what the data tells us.* NPR.org. https://www.npr.org/2022/09/19/1123767437/joe-biden-covid-19-pandemic-over

Baltimore Sun - We are currently unavailable in your region. (n.d.). Retrieved October 12, 2022, from https://www.tribpub.com/gdpr/baltimoresun.com/

Berrien, H. (2022, September 8). *IG Report Blasts Biden's Homeland Security For Improperly Vetting Afghan Refugees.* The Daily Wire. https://www.dailywire.com/news/ig-report-blasts-bidens-homeland-security-for-improperly-vetting-afghan-refugees

biden-tells-charlamagne-tha-god-if-you-dont-support-me-then-you-aint-black/. (n.d.). *Https://Thehill.Com.* https://thehill.com/homenews/campaign/499128-biden-tells-charlamagne-tha-god-if-you-dont-support-me-then-you-aint-black/

Black Votes Matter. (2016, July 26). https://www.creators.com/read/thomas-sowell/07/16/black-votes-matter

REFERENCES

black-students-demand-segregated-spaces. (n.d.). https://www.thecollege fix.com. https://www.thecollegefix.com/black-students-demand-segregated-spaces-white-students/

Blair, L. (2016, May 13). *Pastor Jamal Bryant Breaks Silence on Baby Controversy: "God Ain't Finished With Me."* The Christian Post. https://www.christianpost.com/news/pastor-jamal-bryant-breaks-silence-on-baby-controversy-god-aint-finished-with-me.html

Bloom, L. B. (2022, February 23). *Crime In America: Study Reveals The 10 Most Unsafe Cities (It's Not Where You Think).* Forbes. https://www.forbes.com/sites/laurabegleybloom/2022/02/23/crime-in-america-study-reveals-the-10-most-dangerous-cities-its-not-where-you-think/?sh=575c8d2f7710

brett-favre-scandal-alleged-8-million-welfare-scam-explained. (n.d.). https://www.forbes.com. https://www.forbes.com/sites/marisadellatto/2022/04/13/brett-favre-scandal-alleged-8-million-welfare-scam-explained/?sh=4191890d2ddd

bs-md-cr-linnard-20220807-lq6l7qk2xng5zgrvuvkxg467ny-story.html. (n.d.). https://www.baltimoresun.com. https://www.baltimoresun.com/news/crime/bs-md-cr-linnard-20220807-lq6l7qk2xng5zgrvuvkxg467ny-story.html

Butanis, B. (2022, February 18). *Henrietta Lacks | Her Impact and Our Outreach.* https://www.hopkinsmedicine.org/henriettalacks

Chris-rock-niggas-vs-black-people-.(n.d.).genius.com.https://https://genius.com/Chris-rock-niggas-vs-black-people-annotated

Comedy. (2022, September 30). *Why Bill Burr Never Liked White Woman*. YouTube. https://www.youtube.com/watch?v=5pU3J8nKSxI

crime-in-america-study-reveals-the-10-most-dangerous-cities-its-not-where-you-think/?sh=575c8d2f7710. (n.d.). https://www.forbes.com. https://www.forbes.com/sites/laurabegleybloom/2022/02/23/crime-in-america-study-reveals-the-10-most-dangerous-cities-its-not-where-you-think/?sh=575c8d2f7710

Evans, F. (2022, June 22). *Why Harry Truman Ended Segregation in the US Military in 1948*. HISTORY. https://www.history.com/news/harry-truman-executive-order-9981-desegration-military-1948

Fahrenheit 9/11. (n.d.). MICHAEL MOORE. Retrieved October 13, 2022, from https://michaelmoore.com/movies/fahrenheit-911/

Fearnow, B. (2020, July 7). *Religious Organizations Receive $7.3 Billion in PPP Loans, Megachurches Amass Millions*. Newsweek. https://www.newsweek.com/religious-organizations-receive-73-billion-ppp-loans-megachurches-amass-millions-1515963

Félix, D. st. (2020, June 10). *The Embarrassment of Democrats Wearing Kente-Cloth Stoles*. The New Yorker. https://www.newyorker.com/culture/on-and-off-the-avenue/the-embarrassment-of-democrats-wearing-kente-cloth-stoles

Fox News. (2021, February 24). *Obama says reparations "justified" but "politics of White resistance" made it "nonstarter" to propose*. https://www.foxnews.com/politics/

REFERENCES

obama-springsteen-podcast-reparations-white-resistance

Geary, D. (2021, May 5). *The Moynihan Report: An Annotated Edition*. The Atlantic. https://www.theatlantic.com/politics/archive/2015/09/the-moynihan-report-an-annotated-edition/404632/

Grandmaster Flash & The Furious Five (Ft. Duke Bootee & Grandmaster Melle Mel) – The Message. (n.d.-a). Genius. Retrieved October 13, 2022, from https://genius.com/Grandmaster-flash-and-the-furious-five-the-message-lyrics

Grandmaster Flash & The Furious Five (Ft. Duke Bootee & Grandmaster Melle Mel) – The Message. (n.d.-b). Genius. Retrieved October 13, 2022, from https://genius.com/Grandmaster-flash-and-the-furious-five-the-message-lyrics

HAITIAN BORDER CRISIS AT BOILING POINT | OnlineColumnist.com - Dr. John M. Curtis. (2021, September 19). https://onlinecolumnist.com/2021/09/19/haitian-border-crisis-at-boiling-point/

Harrington, E. (2015, May 4). *Baltimore Received $1.8 Billion from Obama's Stimulus Law*. Washington Free Beacon. https://freebeacon.com/issues/baltimore-received-1-8-billion-from-obamas-stimulus-law/

Hawkins, K. U. T. (2020, July 23). *Remove statues of Margaret Sanger, Planned Parenthood founder tied to eugenics and racism*. USA TODAY. https://eu.usatoday.com/story/opinion/2020/07/23/racism-eugenics-margaret-sanger-deserves-no-honors-column/5480192002/

Henry Louis Gates Jr. (n.d.). AAAS. Retrieved October 11, 2022, from https://aaas.fas.harvard.edu/people/henry-louis-gates-jr

Hersher, R. (2016, September 27). *U.S. Government To Pay $492 Million To 17 American Indian Tribes.* NPR.org. https://www.npr.org/sections/thetwo-way/2016/09/27/495627997/u-s-government-to-pay-492-million-to-17-american-indian-tribes

https://hotair.com/jazz-shaw/2022/08/22/naacp-asks-for-national-guard-to-be-deployed-in-baltimore-. (n.d.). https://hotair.com/jazz-shaw/2022/08/22/naacp-asks-for-national-guard-to-be-deployed-in-baltimore-n491395. https://hotair.com/jazz-shaw/2022/08/22/naacp-asks-for-national-guard-to-be-deployed-in-baltimore-n491395

https://tecartabible.com/share/309/Ephesians+6:5. (n.d.). https://tecartabible.com.https://tecartabible.com/share/309/Ephesians+6:5

https://tecartabible.com/share/309/Matthew+23:9-10. (n.d.). https://tecartabible.com/share/309/Matthew+23:9-10. https://tecartabible.com/share/309/Matthew+23:9-10

https://www.brandonforbaltimore.com. (n.d.). https://www.brandonforbaltimore.com. https://www.brandonforbaltimore.com

Jesse Helms Facts. (n.d.). Encyclopedia Britannica. Retrieved October 12, 2022, from https://www.britannica.com/facts/Jesse-Helms

Kearns, D. (1987). *LYNDON JOHNSON AND THE AMERICAN DREAM Easton Press* (Reprint). Easton Press.

REFERENCES

Kelly, A. (2015, August 14). *Fact Check: Was Planned Parenthood Started To "Control" The Black Population?* NPR.org. https://www.npr.org/sections/itsallpolitics/2015/08/14/432080520/fact-check-was-planned-parenthood-started-to-control-the-black-population

Khia - My Neck, My Back (Lick It) Lyrics | AZLyrics.com. (n.d.). Retrieved October 14, 2022, from https://www.azlyrics.com/lyrics/khia/myneckmybackdirtyversion.html

LaBarbera: Drag Queen Story Hour is 'Indoctrination' of Children Into LGBTQ Culture. (n.d.). CNSNews.com. Retrieved October 9, 2022, from https://www.cnsnews.com/blog/michael-w-chapman/labarbera-drag-queen-story-hour-indoctrination-children-lgbtq-culture

Martinez, E. (2015, February 19). *Bishop Eddie Long Scandal: He Wanted Sex in Church, Says Accuser Jamal Parris.* CBS News. https://www.cbsnews.com/news/bishop-eddie-long-scandal-he-wanted-sex-in-church-says-accuser-jamal-parris/

Muhammad, K. (2020, September 30). *The Contempt of Feminism in the Black Community.* Joshua's Truth. https://joshuastruth.com/2020/09/17/the-contempt-of-feminism-in-the-black-community/

Nadeem, R. (2022, June 16). *1. A brief statistical portrait of U.S. Hispanics.* Pew Research Center Science & Society. https://www.pewresearch.org/science/2022/06/14/a-brief-statistical-portrait-of-u-s-hispanics/

newsone Staff. (2012a, January 16). *What Has Obama Done For You Lately?* NewsOne. https://newsone.com/1797175/barack-obamas-top-five-accomplishments-for-black-america-wiki/

newsone Staff. (2012b, January 16). *What Has Obama Done For You Lately?* NewsOne. https://newsone.com/1797175/barack-obamas-top-five-accomplishments-for-black-america-wiki/

Office of the Mayor. (2021, May 14). Jackson, MS. https://www.jacksonms.gov/departments/office-of-the-mayor/.

Page not found. (n.d.). NewsOne. Retrieved October 9, 2022, from https://newsone.com/1797175/barack-obamas-top-five-accomplishments-for-black-america-wiki/where+are+my+reparations/

-patterson-lawsuit-schools. (n.d.). https://www.baltimoresun.com. https://www.baltimoresun.com

Pinks, W., Pincus, W., & Pincus, W. (1996, November 16). *DRUG DEALER WHO SAID CIA AIDED CONTRA TRAFFICKERS ALTERS CLAIM*. Washington Post. https://www.washingtonpost.com/archive/politics/1996/11/16/drug-dealer-who-said-cia-aided-contra-traffickers-alters-claim/331ce857-0cb5-417d-a8df-4fbae180cfd8/

please-dont-tell-martin. (n.d.). https://https://genius.com/Chris-rock-niggas-vs-black-people-annotated

/pmc/articles/PMC7319652/. (n.d.). https://www.ncbi.nlm.nih.gov. https://www.ncbi.nlm.nih.gov/pmc/articles/PMC7319652/

REFERENCES

Red Springs remembers deadly tornadoes of 1984. (2014, March 28). WRAL.com. https://www.wral.com/red-springs-remembers-deadly-tornadoes-of-1984/13521773/

Reichard, R. (2012, July 16). *The Black Church: How same-sex marriage threatens Obama's re-election.* https://dcspotlight.com/features/living-the-life/the-black-church-how-same-sex-marriage-threatens-obamas-re-election/

remdesivir-shouldn-t-be-used-hospitalized-covid-19-patients-who-n. (n.d.). https://www.nbcnews.com. https://www.nbcnews.com/health/health-news/remdesivir-shouldn-t-be-used-hospitalized-covid-19-patients-who-n1248320

Schmidt, J. (2022, January 10). *Former CBP commissioner: 'We have lost control of the southwest border'* ADN América. https://adnamerica.com/en/united-states/former-cbp-commissioner-we-have-lost-control-southwest-border

Sekulow, J. (n.d.). *What is School Choice?* American Center for Law and Justice. Retrieved October 12, 2022, from https://aclj.org/school-choice/what-is-school-choice

Some Of Martin Luther King Jr.'s Most Radical Statements. (2017, January 16). MintPress News. https://www.mintpressnews.com/some-of-martin-luther-king-jr-s-most-radical-statements/224099/

Staff, W. (2022, June 8). *Report: Baltimore City Public Schools changed more than 12,000 grades from failing to passing.* WMAR 2 News Baltimore. https://www.wmar2news.com/news/local-news/report-baltimore-city-public-schools-changed-more-than-12-000-grades-from-failing-to-passing

the-true-story-of-the-women-warriors-of-dahomey. (n.d.-a). https://www.nationalgeographic.com.https://www.nationalgeographic.com/history/article/the-true-story-of-the-women-warriors-of-dahomey

the-true-story-of-the-women-warriors-of-dahomey. (n.d.-b). https://www.nationalgeographic.com.https://www.nationalgeographic.com/history/article/the-true-story-of-the-women-warriors-of-dahomey

Titus+1:7. (n.d.). https://tecartabible.com. https://tecartabible.com/share/309/Titus+1:7

Top 100 Most Dangerous Cities in America. (2020, January 14). National Council for Home Safety and Security. https://www.alarms.org/top-100-most-dangerous-cities-in-america/

what-obama-actually-said-his-rejection-reparations/. (n.d.). https://www.washingtonpost.com. https://www.washingtonpost.com/politics/2019/07/09/what-obama-actually-said-his-rejection-reparations/

what-obama-actually-said-his-rejection-reparations/. (n.d.). *https://www.washingtonpost.com.https://www.washingtonpost.com/politics/2019/07/09/what-obama-actually-said-his-rejection-reparations(n.d.)https//what-obama-actually-said-his-*ejection-reparations/. (n.d.). https://www.washingtonpost.com. https://www.washingtonpost.com/politics/2019/07/09/what-obama-actually-said-his-rejection-reparations/

REFERENCES

Wikipedia contributors. (2022, October 14). *Dixiecrat*. Wikipedia. https://en.wikipedia.org/wiki/Dixiecrat

Wolf, Z. B. (2021, September 23). *Why many thousands of Haitians converged on the US-Mexico border*. CNN. https://edition.cnn.com/2021/09/22/politics/haitian-immigrants-us-border-explained/index.html

www.charlotteobserver.com/news/politics-government/article68401147.html. (n.d.). www.charlotteobserver.com. https://www.charlotteobserver.com/news/politics-government/article68401147.html

yes-undocumented-immigrants-take-jobs-americans-heres-proof/. (n.d.). *https://www.washingtonpost.com*. https://www.washingtonpost.com/opinions/2019/08/16/yes-undocumented-immigrants-take-jobs-americans-heres-proof/

(2011, October 13). *Michelle Alexander: More Black Men Are In Prison Today Than Were Enslaved In 1850*. HuffPost. https://www.huffpost.com/entry/michelle-alexander-more-black-men-in-prison-slaves-1850_n_1007368

Endnotes

1. bs-md-cr-linnard-20220807-lq6l7qk2xng5zgrvuvkxg-467ny-story.html, n.d.
2. https://nubianmoor.blogspot.com/2006/02/please-dont-tell-martin.html. please-dont-tell-martin. (n.d.). Nubianmoor.
3. https://genius.com/Chris-rock-niggas-vs-black-people-annotated
4. https://www.thecollegefix.com/black-students-demand-segregated-spaces-white-students/
5. https://www.nationalgeographic.com/history/article/the-true-story-of-the-women-warriors-of-dahomey
6. Khia - My Neck, My Back (Lick It) Lyrics | AZLyrics.com, n.d.
7. Grandmaster Flash & the Furious Five (Ft. Duke Bootee & Grandmaster Melle Mel) – the Message, n.d.-b
8. https://www.nationalgeographic.com/history/article/the-true-story-of-the-women-warriors-of-dahomey
9. Africa-during-the-scramble-the-amazon-s-last-stand, n.d.
10. https://www.theatlantic.com/politics/archive/2015/09/the-moynihan-report-an-annotated-edition/404632/
11. https://www.scribbr.com/citation/generator/folders/6zCLLQckvq2hOic2c4Y0vF/lists/7J5B9Q0TCYaPKG4ijYlEgV/sources/6hvluCjHu4zpUMsMqBlBUk/
12. *Some Of Martin Luther King Jr.'s Most Radical Statements.*

	(2017, January 16). MintPress News. Retrieved October 9, 2022, from https://www.mintpressnews.com/some-of-martin-luther-king-jr-s-most-radical-statements/224099/
13	Muhammad, K. (2020, September 30). *The Contempt of Feminism in the Black Community.* Joshua's Truth. Retrieved October 9, 2022, from https://joshuastruth.com/2020/09/17/the-contempt-of-feminism-in-the-black-community/
14	Comedy, 2022
15	Nadeem, 2022
16	Hawkins, 2020
17	Applications Open for Baltimore's Guaranteed Income Pilot Program, 2022
18	8 Important Statistics That Black America Needs to Recognize Now, 2011
19	(2011, October 13). *Michelle Alexander: More Black Men Are In Prison Today Than Were Enslaved In 1850.* HuffPost. Retrieved October 9, 2022, from https://www.huffpost.com/entry/michelle-alexander-more-black-men-in-prison-slaves-1850_n_1007368
20	Remdesivir-shouldn-t-be-used-hospitalized-covid-19-patients-who-n, n.d.
21	Archie, 2022b
22	Fearnow, 2020
23	Butanis, 2022
24	Pmc/Articles/PMC7319652/, n.d.
25	Archie, 2022
26	(LaBarbera: Drag Queen Story Hour Is 'Indoctrination' of Children Into LGBTQ Culture, n.d.)
27	*https://www.brandonforbaltimore.com.* (n.d.). https://www.brandonforbaltimore.com. https://www.brandonforbaltimore.com

ENDNOTES

28 Top 100 Most Dangerous Cities in America, 2020
29 Crime-in-america-study-reveals-the-10-most-dangerous-cities-its-not-where-you-think/?Sh=575c8d2f7710, n.d.
30 Fahrenheit 9/11, n.d.
31 Office of the Mayor, 2021
32 Blair, L. (2016, May 13). *Pastor Jamal Bryant Breaks Silence on Baby Controversy: "God Ain't Finished With Me."* The Christian Post. Retrieved October 9, 2022, from https://www.christianpost.com/news/pastor-jamal-bryant-breaks-silence-on-baby-controversy-god-aint-finished-with-me.html
33 Martinez, E. (2015, February 19). *Bishop Eddie Long Scandal: He Wanted Sex in Church, Says Accuser Jamal Parris.* CBS News. Retrieved October 9, 2022, from https://www.cbsnews.com/news/bishop-eddie-long-scandal-he-wanted-sex-in-church-says-accuser-jamal-parris/
34 Titus+1:7, n.d.
35 https://tecartabible.com/share/309/Matthew+23:9-10, n.d.
36 https://tecartabible.com/share/309/Matthew+23:9-10, n.d.
37 https://tecartabible.com/share/309/Ephesians+6:5, n.d.
38 Brett-favre-scandal-alleged-8-million-welfare-scam-explained, n.d.
39 newsone Staff, 2012b
40 Fox News, 2021
41 What-obama-actually-said-his-rejection-reparations/, n.d.
42 Hersher, 2016
43 (Reichard, 2012)
44 https://dcspotlight.com/features/living-the-life/the-black-church-how-same-sex-marriage-threatens-obamas-re-election/, 2012
45 *www.charlotteobserver.com/news/politics-government/article68401147.html*. (n.d.).

46 *Red Springs Remembers Deadly Tornadoes of 1984, 2014*
47 Henry Louis Gates Jr., n.d.
48 Félix, 2020
49 African-slave-castles.html, n.d.
50 Berrien, 2022
51 HAITIAN BORDER CRISIS AT BOILING POINT | OnlineColumnist.com - Dr. John M. Curtis, 2021
52 (Wolf, 2021)
53 (Schmidt, 2022)
54 "Yes-undocumented-immigrants-take-jobs-americans-heres-proof/," n.d.
55 Black Votes Matter, 2016
56 Jesse Helms Facts, n.d.
57 Wikipedia contributors, 2022
58 Access Denied, 2012b
59 Evans, 2022
60 ("Biden-tells-charlamagne-tha-god-if-you-dont-support-me-then-you-aint-black/," n.d.)
61 Harrington, 2015
62 https://hotair.com/jazz-shaw/2022/08/22/naacp-asks-for-national-guard-to-be-deployed-in-baltimore-, n.d.
63 Pincus et al., 1996
64 -patterson-lawsuit-schools, n.d.
65 Staff, 2022
66 Sekulow, n.d.

AMPLIFLUENCE
AMPLIFY YOUR INFLUENCE

You're the Expert, but are you struggling to Monetize your Authority?

Amplify Your Influence in 3 Sessions

Speak Your Message

Publish Your Message

Convert Your Message

Check Out All Of Our 'Live' Tour Stops

Authors and Speakers often find themselves struggling to build a strategy that actually makes them money.

amplifluence.com

SCAN FOR TOUR INFO

More Books From Perfect Publishing

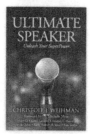

www.PerfectPublishing.com

More Books From Perfect Publishing

 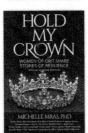  
   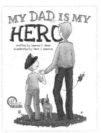 

www.PerfectPublishing.com

Made in the USA
Middletown, DE
25 March 2023